T0323576

Cambridge Elements ≡

Elements in England in the Early Medieval World
edited by
Megan Cavell
University of Birmingham
Rory Naismith
University of Cambridge
Winfried Rudolf
University of Göttingen
Emily V. Thornbury
Yale University

RECOVERING OLD ENGLISH

Kees Dekker
University of Groningen

CAMBRIDGE
UNIVERSITY PRESS

Shaftesbury Road, Cambridge CB2 8EA, United Kingdom

One Liberty Plaza, 20th Floor, New York, NY 10006, USA

477 Williamstown Road, Port Melbourne, VIC 3207, Australia

314–321, 3rd Floor, Plot 3, Splendor Forum, Jasola District Centre,
New Delhi – 110025, India

103 Penang Road, #05–06/07, Visioncrest Commercial, Singapore 238467

Cambridge University Press is part of Cambridge University Press & Assessment,
a department of the University of Cambridge.

We share the University's mission to contribute to society through the pursuit of
education, learning and research at the highest international levels of excellence.

www.cambridge.org
Information on this title: www.cambridge.org/9781009478809

DOI: 10.1017/9781009371681

When citing this work, please include a reference to the DOI 10.1017/9781009371681

First published 2024

A catalogue record for this publication is available from the British Library.

ISBN 978-1-009-47880-9 Hardback
ISBN 978-1-009-37169-8 Paperback
ISSN 2632-203X (online)
ISSN 2632-2021 (print)

Recovering Old English

Elements in England in the Early Medieval World

DOI: 10.1017/9781009371681
First published online: January 2024

Kees Dekker
University of Groningen
Author for correspondence: Kees Dekker, c.dekker@rug.nl

Abstract: *Recovering Old English* examines the philological activities of scholars involved in the recovery of Old English in the period between circa 1550 and circa 1830. The discussion focuses on four philological pursuits that dominated this recovery: collecting documents, recording the lexicon, editing texts and studying the grammar. This Element demonstrates that throughout the vicissitudes of history these four components of humanist philology have formed the backbone of Old English studies and constitute a thread that connects the efforts of early modern philologists with the global interest in Old English that we see today.

This Element also has a video abstract: www.cambridge.org/Dekker

Keywords: Old English, Anglo-Saxonism, Old English Dictionaries, Old English Grammars, Antiquarianism

ISBNs: 9781009478809 (HB), 9781009371698 (PB), 9781009371681 (OC)
ISSNs: 2632-203X (online), 2632-2021 (print)

Contents

1 Preamble

Old English is the vernacular language spoken and written in much of what is now England and southern Scotland during the early Middle Ages. It evolved from the dialects of West Germanic tribes which settled in areas of mainland Britain in the 5th and 6th centuries. Referred to as Angles, Saxons and Jutes by the Venerable Bede, the period's most eminent historian, these tribes have become known collectively as Anglo-Saxons or as the early English. Over time, their language has been known as 'Saxon', 'Anglo-Saxon' and 'English-Saxon', but since the 1960s the term 'Old English' (OE) has prevailed. Written records of OE testify to a rich culture of vernacular literacy in England from the 7th to the 11th centuries. An accelerating sequence of demographic, social and linguistic changes in the 9th, 10th and 11th centuries – most notably the settlement of Scandinavians, who spoke related North Germanic dialects, and the regime changes following the conquest of England in 1066 by Norman knights who predominantly used a dialect of French – affected spoken English to such an extent that manuscripts from the middle of the 12th century contain a type of English that linguists have classified as early Middle English. In the vibrant, mobile and more urbanised culture of the later Middle Ages, Middle English developed so rapidly that OE texts became arcane and gradually ceased to be copied. In the 13th and 14th centuries, some OE texts were glossed by individual users to ensure a basic understanding.[1] Ultimately, at the beginning of what we now call the early modern period (beginning c. 1450–1500), texts written in OE were by and large no longer understandable to readers of English, who, as the printer William Caxton reported, thought it resembled German.[2] By the time of King Henry VIII's accession (1509), knowledge of OE, if it existed at all, was incidental, individual, incomplete and inconspicuous.

Paradoxically, Henry VIII's reign would witness the first signs of an emerging interest in OE and in the documents written in that language, and by the end of the Tudor period (1603), the study of OE had gained a foothold in circles of humanist philologists, most notably those associated with the nascent English Church. Remarkably, this interest in OE emerged not only in England but also, albeit on a lesser scale, on the European Continent, particularly in Germany and the Low Countries, where OE was considered a closely related Germanic language. In the subsequent centuries, the early modern interest in OE grew from a humanist fringe activity in the 16th century to a scientific discipline by the second quarter of the 19th. By that time, new generations of dictionaries and grammars of OE were appearing, critical editions of OE texts were becoming available and, most importantly, the scholarly discourse began to include the

---

[1] Treharne, 'English in the Post-Conquest Period'.   [2] Baugh and Cable, *A History*, 191.

scientific methodological principles that are still with us today. It is, therefore, in the period from circa 1550 to circa 1830 that documents written in OE were first collected and described in lists and catalogues. Some of these texts were edited and published in printed volumes, sometimes, but not always, with Latin or English translations. Simultaneously, the OE lexicon was more systematically recorded, first in handwritten glossaries and subsequently in printed dictionaries. In the wake of a more intense engagement with the lexis of texts, the grammar of OE began to be studied: scholars experimented in surveys of the phonology, morphology, lexicology, etymology, onomastics, poetics and dialectology of OE.[3]

This Element explores these philological activities of scholars involved in the recovery of OE in the period between circa 1550 and circa 1830 by examining approaches to documents, language and texts, starting from the four processes to which I have already referred: collecting, recording, editing and studying OE. The developments in these four processes are essential for our understanding of how the knowledge of OE was restored, how its lexicon and grammar gradually came to be understood, and how texts written in OE met with their early modern audiences. I will conclude with a preview of the transition from pre-modern to modern philology in the early 19th century. Each section provides readers with a set of stepping stones which will facilitate further explorations and new inroads. Unavoidable in an Element like this, the number of names is substantial; in all but a few cases I give dates, therefore, to allow quick reference to biographical compendia such as the *Oxford Dictionary of National Biography (ODNB)*. The printed books section in the bibliography of primary sources provides a timeline of major achievements.[4]

Using the term 'philology' requires clarification because of its semantic volatility, as analysed by Haruko Momma. Guiding the reader through a maze of interpretations, Momma concludes that philology 'has no essential character except its love of λόγος', and comprises all text-critical activities undertaken by people who call themselves philologists.[5] What did 'philology' mean for scholars from the 16th to the 18th centuries? Originally meaning 'love of learning' in ancient Greek and Latin, philology came to mean 'explanation or interpretation of the writing of others' in later Latin.[6] These two meanings are complementary, in that the interpretation and explanation of the written texts was regarded as the key to all learning. Philologists were scholars whose love of learning materialised in collecting, reading, editing and explaining texts and

---

[3] Gneuss, *English Language Scholarship*, provides an introduction to the study of English, including OE, with helpful bibliographies.

[4] See pp. 69–72.   [5] Momma, *From Philology to English Studies*, 26.

[6] Lewis and Short, *A Latin Dictionary*, s.v. *philologia*.

languages, who regarded language as the key to learning and who gave particular prominence to words.

For early modern European scholars of OE, philology was both an attitude and a practice, for which they drew inspiration from two major movements of the period: Renaissance humanism and the Protestant Reformation. Humanism, in the words of Nicholas Mann, is

> that concern with the legacy of antiquity – and in particular, but not exclusively, with its literary legacy – which characterises the work of scholars from at least the ninth century onwards. It involves above all the rediscovery and study of ancient Greek and Roman texts, the restoration and interpretation of them and the assimilation of the ideas and values that they contain. It ranges from an archaeological interest in the remains of the past to the details of all manner of written records – from inscriptions to epic poems – but comes to pervade ... almost all areas of post-medieval culture, including theology, philosophy, political thought, jurisprudence, medicine, mathematics and the creative arts.[7]

All philological activities connected with the study of OE during the early modern period fall within the paradigm of Renaissance humanism: the intellectual spirit associated with the recovery of Latin and Greek which began in 14th-century Italy and expanded to the recovery of the vernaculars once it crossed the Alps.

The importance of vernacular texts in north-western Europe was reinforced by the Protestant Reformation. In England, the Reformation became official in 1534 when parliament passed the first Act of Supremacy, which made King Henry VIII head of the English Church.[8] From the beginning, vernacularity was a key tenet in Protestant doctrine, furthering the study of the Bible in newly produced vernacular translations such as those by Martin Luther and William Tyndale, while at the same time embracing the humanist zeal to read and study the originals in Greek, Hebrew and other languages accredited with antiquity. In England, a series of acts from the reign of Edward VI stipulated that the vernacular should be used in prayer, worship and religious study.[9] Protestants pointed to the biblical texts in early Germanic vernaculars, then recently rediscovered by humanist scholars, as support for the legitimacy of their stance. The predominance of Protestants among the early students of OE does not mean that Catholics were not involved, as we will see in the work of Richard Rowlands

---

[7] Mann, 'The Origins', 2.

[8] The first Act of Supremacy was repealed during the reign of Mary I (1553–58), after which a second, slightly adapted version was passed for her sister Elizabeth.

[9] Frantzen, *Desire*, 37.

Verstegan (1548x50–1640), a Catholic Englishman of Dutch origins who had taken refuge in the Spanish Netherlands (see Figure 1).[10]

The historiography of OE studies – its motivations, methods, events, successes and disappointments – is an international and interdisciplinary field. In the 19th century, this history began to be regarded as an important cultural and historical phenomenon in its own right, resulting in publications on this topic. The first attempt at a synthesis was James Ingram's inaugural lecture to the Rawlinsonian professorship of Anglo-Saxon at Oxford (1807), written from a patriotic angle to prove that OE had been 'uninterruptedly cultivated and

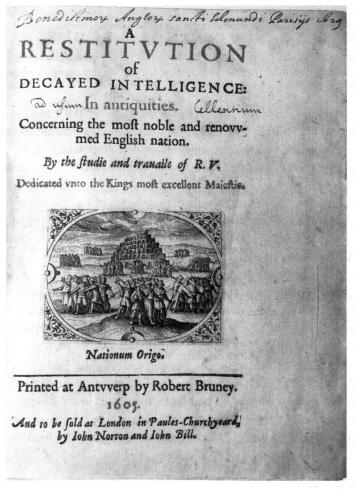

Figure 1 Verstegan, *A Restitution of Decayed Intelligence*, frontispiece

---

continued to this day'.[11] Five Rawlinsonian professors later, Robert Meadows White published a more elaborate account as an introduction to his 1852 edition of the *Ormulum*.[12] Left unmentioned by White is the *Historical Sketch of the Progress and Present State of Anglo-Saxon Literature in England*, published in 1840 by the bookseller and bibliophile John Petheram, which contains the first book-length historiographical study of OE scholarship. The first modern survey is Eleanor N. Adams's *OE Scholarship in England from 1566–1800*, a seminal PhD thesis (Yale University) published in 1917, combining historical, prosopographical and bibliographical information with appendices including extracts from correspondence and prefaces, and an essay on printing OE. Adams's work was of great inspirational value to subsequent publications and, in its holistic purpose, was replaced only in 2015 by John D. Niles's *The Idea of Anglo-Saxon England 1066–1901: Remembering, Forgetting, Deciphering and Renewing the Past*, in which Niles also included the high Middle Ages, the 19th century and the interest in OE in the United States. Niles's outstanding history is organised chronologically and contains a wealth of information on the various traditions, actors, ideas and publications. Chronologically between Adams and Niles stands Allen J. Frantzen's *Desire for Origins: New Language, OE and Teaching the Tradition*, published in 1990, which enriched and transformed research into the history of OE studies by reviewing it in the context of critical theory. Frantzen's work not only answered modern questions about the relevance of the history of a discipline but also opened up new avenues of research by adding a literary dimension, in which early modern scholars were discussed as gatekeepers whose actions and decisions determined the reception of texts, thereby shaping the readers' view of the past.[13] The number and range of publications on the history of OE studies is very substantial, with the long list of recent, outstanding works by Timothy Graham ranking most prominently in a bibliography of well over 800 secondary sources which I compiled for this project.[14]

It is generally acknowledged that most early modern scholars were driven by nationalistic and religious motivations, and studied OE in relation to connecting interests (history, law, theology, geography, literature, languages and arts). They were referred to as antiquaries, 'persons who study or are interested in the past or its remains; persons who study or collect antiquities', whereby an antiquity could be anything from a word or a text to a coin or artefact.[15] Only in the late 18th century did the English antiquary Daines Barrington (1727/8–1800) use the term 'Anglo-Saxonist' for the first time to label scholars 'engaged in the

---

[11] Ingram, *An Inaugural Lecture*, 3.   [12] White, *The Ormulum*, iii–lxii.
[13] Frantzen, *Desire*, 160–1.   [14] References here are, necessarily, selective and brief.
[15] *OED*, s.v. *antiquarian*.

study of the language, literature, history or material remains of the Anglo-Saxon period'.[16] Recently, the term 'Anglo-Saxonist' has come under increased scrutiny by a new generation of students and scholars in a movement to redress 'accepted' ideas about history, ethnography, nationhood and empire.[17] The diverse viewpoints are best illustrated by two interpretations. One defines Anglo-Saxonism as 'the process through which a self-conscious national and racial identity first came into being among the early peoples of the region that we now call England and how, over time, through both scholarly and popular promptings, that identity was transformed into an originary myth available to a wide variety of political and social interests'.[18] Another defines it as 'a set of interrelated and interdependent processes in which [18th-century] contemporaries made use of the Anglo-Saxon period, for ends that were at various moments and for various reasons scholarly, artistic, political, social or cultural, and bound up with the closely related processes involved in any attempt to define a historically grounded English identity'.[19] Whichever perspective one takes, there can be no doubt that in many instances the study of the 'Saxon', 'Anglo-Saxon', 'English-Saxon' or 'English' past was ethnically, culturally, historically, theologically and linguistically biased. As classical humanism presupposed a golden age of Roman and Greek antiquity, so vernacular humanism constructed the idea of a glorious, ancient past that was worthy of veneration. An aspect of that past, the study of language was, at times, abused as a means of positioning the Us against the Other, the superior against the inferior. While this Element approaches the study of OE from a philological angle, it is important to realise that during the early modern period, and also later, the study of language and texts often served to confirm or reinforce the social, political and religious ideas of those who claimed the privilege of owning the past.[20]

2 Collecting Old English

Collection, in the sense of gathering documents (manuscripts and printed books), texts and artefacts with the aim of furthering knowledge and learning, was a core activity of humanist scholarship and one that was foundational for the study of OE during the early modern period. The early modern scholars who recovered OE were in various ways collectors of the materials they studied and published. Collection as a scholarly activity should not be equated with ownership of documents, although the two sometimes go hand-in-hand. Much more, it precedes the realisation of a scholarly aim: a critical edition, a history or

---

[16] Frazier Wood, *Anglo-Saxonism*, xiii.

[17] For one of the most recent contributions, see Wilton, 'What Do We Mean by Anglo-Saxon?'

[18] Frantzen and Niles, 'Introduction', 1.   [19] Frazier Wood, *Anglo-Saxonism*, 3.

[20] Niles, *The Idea*, especially the preface.

chronicle, a dictionary or a catalogue of texts and manuscripts – all start with the accumulation of documents and data. This section will explore activities of collection in the history of OE studies.

Manuscripts containing OE have seen a turbulent history. In his 1957 *Catalogue of Manuscripts Containing Anglo-Saxon* and the Supplement published in 1976, the palaeographer and codicologist Neil Ker listed 421 'literary' manuscripts containing OE written in England before around 1200 and a further forty-five manuscripts of OE written by foreign scribes. Ker's numbering of these manuscripts has been in use ever since.[21] Before the 16th century, nearly all of these manuscripts in Britain were stored in monastic or cathedral libraries. Very few of those are still owned by the same institutions; the best known is perhaps Exeter, Cathedral Library 3501 (116), the Exeter Book of OE poetry, which had been donated to the library by Bishop Leofric before his death in 1072.[22] While OE continued to be read, and while in Worcester Cathedral texts were studied and glossed in the 13th century by a scribe known as 'the Tremulous Hand',[23] evidence of the study of OE in the 14th and 15th centuries is very scarce,[24] and manuscripts containing OE were presumably deemed to be of little value. A late 13th- or early 14th-century hand wrote in CUL Ii. I. 33 (18) that this storehouse of sermons in English was 'not valued because of unknown language'.[25] Despite the apparent lack of appreciation, monastic and institutional libraries remained the custodians of most manuscripts containing OE until the Reformation. This stable ownership changed in the wake of Henry VIII's Dissolution of religious houses between 1535 and 1540, when the contents of many monastic libraries were dispersed, with books being destroyed or ending up in the hands of wealthy members of the gentry to whom the dissolved religious houses were sold.[26] The accounts of some manuscripts illustrate the disinterest in these turbulent years. In 1566, CUL Ii. 4. 6, an 11th-century manuscript of Ælfric's *Catholic Homilies*, was discovered together with a batch of others at the former Benedictine abbey of Tavistock, Devonshire, by Robert Ferrar, a servant of the second Earl of Bedford, whose family had owned the disused abbey for more than twenty-five years. All that time, the manuscripts must have stood there, unnoticed.

Most evidence from the turbulent decades following the Dissolution comes from the records of English antiquarians and historians such as John Leland

---

[21] In this section, references to manuscripts are supplied with Ker's numbers within parentheses.

[22] See Ker, *Medieval Libraries*, for the provenances and current ownerships from British libraries. Exeter manuscripts containing OE are discussed by Graham, 'The Early Modern Afterlife'.

[23] Franzen, *The Tremulous Hand*; Niles, *The Idea*, 35–9.

[24] Graham, 'The Beginnings of Old English Studies', 29.

[25] Ker, *Catalogue*, 23: 'non appreciatum propter ydioma incognitum'.

[26] See Wright, 'The Dispersal of Libraries', 149–52; Carley, 'The Dispersal'; Niles, *The Idea*, 50–1; and Ker, *Catalogue*, 562–7, for private ownership.

(1506–52) and John Bale (1495–1563), who, in the 16th century, catalogued and collected books in England. The former was a royal chaplain, poet and antiquary by vocation, who, according to his own assertions, had received a commission from King Henry VIII in 1533 to collect from monastic and institutional libraries those books which were of importance.[27] Within a number of itineraries Leland not only catalogued but also collected books in the libraries he visited.[28] Leland seems to have owned a manuscript of Asser's *Life of King Alfred* (171) with some OE charms, used BL, Cotton Tiberius B. i, containing the OE *Orosius* (191), the verse *Menologium* and the *A-S Chronicle*, and annotated the Latin texts in manuscripts which also contained OE: Cambridge, Trinity College R. 7. 28 (770) (88), BL, Cotton Vitellius A. xix (217) and OBL, Auct. F. 2 .14 (295). Although Leland's reputation as a scholar of OE has recently been downplayed by Graham,[29] his knowledge of the whereabouts and contents of manuscripts in the period around the Dissolution was presumably unparalleled and was the reason in 1549 for his friend and fellow bibliographer John Bale to publish Leland's account of early itineraries, which had been presented to Henry VIII as a *New Yeare's Gift* in 1534.

Bale's comments on the fates of English books and libraries in the decades following the Dissolution are our main source of information about book destruction, exportation of books and a widely disparate ownership.[30] For manuscripts containing OE, Bale's information is confirmed by Ker's 'Index of Owners', which paints a picture of 16th-century ownership, displaying prominent figures such as William Bowier, the Keeper of Records in the Tower, William Cecil, Queen Elizabeth's Secretary of State, Henry Fitzalan, the Earl of Arundel, as well as completely unknown owners such as Thomas Aynesworth, whose name appears on fol. 1 of Durham Cathedral Library, B. III. 32 (107), a manuscript that changed hands several times before it ended up in Durham.[31] The list of owners in Ker's 'Index' also confirms Bale's report of manuscripts leaving England, some of which ended up with the first generation of continental humanists interested in OE. In 1572 the French lawyer and polymath François Pithou (1543–1621) acquired a manuscript (now lost) in Oxford and took it back with him to France; it included works by Bede and a section of Ælfric's *Glossary*.[32] Another manuscript of similar material (406) once belonged to Marcus Welser of Augsburg (1558–1614).[33] One or more manuscripts from Abingdon (now Antwerp, Plantin

---

[27] Graham, 'Anglo-Saxon Studies', 416; Carley, 'The Dispersal', 273–5.
[28] Carley, 'The Dispersal', 276–80.   [29] Graham, 'Anglo-Saxon Studies', 416.
[30] Graham and Watson, *The Recovery of the Past*, 17–53, 'John Bale's Letter to Matthew Parker, 30 July 1560'.
[31] Ker, *Catalogue*, 562–9.
[32] Rudolf and Pelle, 'Friedrich Lindenbrog's Old English Glossaries', 622–4.   [33] *Ibid.* 624–5.

Moretus Museum, 16.2 and 16.8, BL, Add. 32246 (2, 3) and Brussels, Bibliothèque Royale, 1650 (1520) (8)) ended up in Flanders, perhaps before 1562.[34] Ker's 'Index' also reveals increased ownership of OE manuscripts among the gentry, whose role as owners and readers of books had increased in the 15th century. John Apsley of Thakeham, who owned BL, Royal 7 C. IV (256), was an MP, while Thomas Augustine Styward, who owned OBL, Bodley 130 (302), a herbal from Bury St Edmunds, was mayor of Norwich. Sixteenth-century owners also included women: a certain Barbara Crokker owned BL, Harley 585 (231), another herbal and medicinal codex. The name of 'Margaret Rollesleye', once with the epithet 'wydowe', is inscribed six times on pages 130–31 of CCCC 422 (70), known as the Red Book of Darley. The freedom she felt to mark up the manuscript suggests entitlement, if not ownership.[35] The records of 16th-century ownership also provide evidence of the revaluation of manuscripts containing OE. Several of the owners mentioned by Ker who inscribed their names in the manuscripts are members of the gentry with intellectual, antiquarian interests, including the mathematician Thomas Allen (1542–1632), the administrator and diplomat Robert Beale (1541–1601), the mathematician and astrologer John Dee (1527–1608) and the diplomat and author Daniel Rogers (c. 1538–91). The most significant of them all was the clergyman Robert Talbot (c. 1505–58), of whom Ker states that he was 'the first person, so far as we know', to collect *and read* manuscripts containing OE after the Dissolution. Ker lists nine manuscripts which Talbot used for his OE studies (17, 45, 148, 151, 164, 191, 209, 312, 360), stating that 'there is no reason to doubt that in his case use implies possession'.[36] Graham makes a convincing case for Talbot's ownership of two additional manuscripts (23, 142), while transcripts in his hand suggest that he had access to manuscripts which have since then disappeared.[37] The true extent of Talbot's work on OE has emerged only recently as a result of detailed bibliographical studies which show him to be a pivotal figure in the first phase of OE scholarship, who was motivated by a strong interest in history and antiquarianism.[38] Talbot is, perhaps, the first scholar of OE for whom collection was a deliberate aspect of his study of OE, involving not only manuscripts but also texts and their contents, as his underlinings of names and place names indicate. Nevertheless, much is still unclear about the plights of

---

[34] Bremmer and Dekker, *Manuscripts in the Low Countries*, 2.

[35] Ker, *Catalogue*, 121. Budney, *Insular, Anglo-Saxon and Anglo-Norman Manuscript Art*, I, 648–9, has identified her as Margaret, the widow of John Rollesley, from Darley in Derbyshire who died in 1562.

[36] Ker, *Catalogue*, l.

[37] Graham, 'Robert Talbot's "Old Saxonice Bede"', 297–304; Graham, 'Early Modern Users', 271–9.

[38] References to Talbot's efforts are often linked with those of the Welsh mathematician Robert Recorde (c. 1512–58), who borrowed manuscripts from Talbot for his antiquarian work.

manuscripts during the decades following the Dissolution. The recent discoveries of parchment strips in modern book bindings that were cut from a manuscript of Ælfric's first series of *Catholic Homilies* and a Winchester psalter with OE glosses corroborate Bale's reports of book destruction during the fundamentalist reigns of Edward VI and Mary I.[39] At the same time, we see that eventually almost all surviving manuscripts of OE ended up with dedicated collectors.

A new chapter in the history of collection was written by Matthew Parker (1504–75), archbishop of Canterbury from 1559 to 1575, and his circle of collaborators. Whereas Leland, Bale and Talbot had been pioneers exploring the field, Parker led the main column that put OE on the map for good. Parker received recognition for this remarkable feat during his own lifetime, and it has never waned since. There is a rich bibliography of studies on Parker's motivations, influence and achievements. His collecting efforts have been discussed in detail by, most notably, C. E. Wright, Raymond Page, Timothy Graham and Anthony Grafton, of which Page and Graham offer detailed analyses of Parker's books and manuscripts and pay most attention to OE.[40] The rich *ODNB* entry on Parker is provided with an extensive bibliography, which also illustrates the many other qualities of Parker as a theologian and politician. As Graham observes in 2008: 'during the years of Parker's archiepiscopate, more than 500 manuscripts passed into his hands', and many more printed books, which have been related to more than 'forty religious houses and secular institutions'.[41] One of Parker's incentives was a request made by the Lutheran reformer Matthias Flacius Illyricus (1520–75) to Queen Elizabeth to supply him with materials about church history and church councils. Parker organised a search for manuscripts to satisfy Flacius's interests, which coincided in many ways with his own,[42] because as archbishop of the Protestant English Church Parker likewise wished to provide ancient examples for its doctrines, history and, most of all, independence. At the same time, as Graham warns us, it is possible to overemphasise the polemical incentives of Parker and his group,[43] as they were also driven by an interest in English history beyond that of the English Church. From the very beginning, therefore, manuscripts containing OE nourished English religious and political sentiments. Aware of John Bale's efforts in the field of bibliography, Parker contacted Bale for support in 1560. Bale's long letter to Parker,

---

[39] Porck, 'Newly Discovered Pieces'.

[40] Wright, 'The Dispersal of Monastic Libraries'; Page, 'The Parker Register'; Page, *Matthew Parker*; Graham, 'Matthew Parker's Manuscripts'; Graham, 'The Beginnings'; Grafton, 'Matthew Parker'.

[41] Graham, 'Matthew Parker's Manuscripts', 322, 327.

[42] Graham and Watson, *The Recovery of the Past*, 2–5.

[43] Graham, 'Matthew Parker's Manuscripts', 422.

preserved in CUL, Add. 7489, reveals that Parker's collecting efforts were part of a wider humanist effort comprising not just manuscripts of OE but also texts in Latin.[44] It seems, though, as if the first decade of his archiepiscopacy opened his eyes to OE. In July 1568 his agents received royal authorisation to search out and peruse books and documents that were important to the realm, but donors also took the initiative and sent him books, as witnessed by his correspondence. Many of these manuscripts were entirely or partly in OE. The effect of Parker's collecting efforts was the beginning of a *translatio collectionis*, from monastic libraries, via a disparate ownership in the middle of the 16th century, into more centralised collections.

The lasting importance of collection is its record or archive left to posterity, and in this respect Parker excelled. His register of books donated in 1574 to the library of Corpus Christi College, Cambridge, counts as one of the most important English bibliographical documents from this period, even though, as Page has indicated, its value as a reflection of Parker's own collection is doubtful, as books were lost and sometimes replaced.[45] Similarly revealing of the early stages of collection is the list of writers on medieval English history drawn up by Parker's Latin secretary and collaborator, John Joscelyn (1529–1603).[46] Most important, however, for the study of OE is the bestowal of Parker's books to the Library of Corpus Christi College and Cambridge University Library, a combined legacy forming a collection that has been at the centre of OE studies ever since Parker died. The real extent of OE texts that passed through his hands may never be known, however, because Parker was clearly selective in his collecting efforts. Of three OE manuscripts sent to him in 1566 by John Scory, the bishop of Hereford, two have not been identified: a *Vita sancti Marcellini* and a *Vite quorundam sanctorum*.[47] In addition, the invasive treatment of some manuscripts in Parker's custody, which could involve erasure of text or replacement of folios or entire quires, may have led to losses that we are now unaware of.[48]

Anthony Grafton states that 'Parker established two basic habits: that of doing elaborate research into the richest sources he could find . . . and that of collaborating with a secretary or assistant'.[49] In fact, the two could be merged, in that Parker employed or inspired a circle of antiquarian talents who shared his ideas and views and put his library to work. Some of them were also involved in collection, albeit on a smaller scale. Parker's son John (1548–1619) inherited some of his father's OE manuscripts and acquired

---

[44] Edited in Graham and Watson, *The Recovery of the Past*, 17–53.
[45] Page, 'The Parker Register', 14.
[46] Edited in Graham and Watson, *The Recovery of the Past*, 55–109.
[47] Graham, 'Matthew Parker's Manuscripts', 325.   [48] *Ibid.* 328–36.
[49] Grafton, 'Matthew Parker', 25; Niles, *The Idea*, 55–6.

some others, which are now in the Library of Trinity College, Cambridge.[50]
John Joscelyn annotated and used many of Parker's manuscripts for these studies,
but also possessed the legal codex that is now BL, Cotton Nero A. i, and
(presumably) five others, none of which entered Parker's collection.[51] Together
with two fellow antiquarians, Laurence Nowell (1530–c. 1570) and William
Lambarde (1536–1601), Joscelyn was also engaged in another aspect of collection: transcribing OE texts. As tutor in the household of William Cecil, Laurence
Nowell was a voracious reader of OE manuscripts, which he copied and collated
in a clear Anglo-Saxon minuscule hand (see Figure 2). One of his focal interests

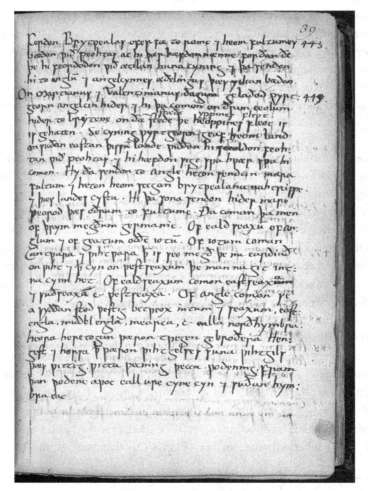

Figure 2 London, British Library, Cotton Domitian A. xviii, f. 39r

---

[50] Ker, *Catalogue*, 566.   [51] Graham, 'Anglo-Saxon Studies', 422; Ker, *Catalogue*, 565.

concerned the *Anglo-Saxon Chronicle*, an interest he shared with Joscelyn. The result of their labours illustrates the intensity with which they studied and transcribed the medieval originals.[52] Laurence Nowell's transcripts from medieval manuscripts were also the basis for William Lambarde's edition of the laws in OE (1568), and it was Nowell who supplied Lambarde in 1565 with a transcript of Ælfric's *Grammar* and *Glossary* (London, Westminster Abbey, MS 30).[53] Together with Nowell and Lambarde, the Parker circle thus added another dimension to collection by transcribing and collating OE texts. Transcripts were not the equivalent of our modern scanner, mobile phone or microfilm; instead, they allowed transcribers to compile and edit as they went along, and in some cases constitute a link in the chain between medieval manuscripts and printed books.

The interest in collection remained important to subsequent generations of antiquarians, as can be seen from two other major collections of manuscripts that played a pivotal role in the beginnings of OE studies. The more important of these was the Cotton Library, whose history began in 1588, when Sir Robert (Bruce) Cotton (1571–1631), a young enthusiastic, fortunate collector, acquired his first three manuscripts (of which one contained OE); he went on to assemble the most important collection of manuscripts containing OE, including treasures such as the *Beowulf* manuscript and the Lindisfarne Gospels.[54] The foundation of Cotton's library should be linked to that of the Elizabethan Society of Antiquaries, some two years earlier. Its members, including Cotton, discussed antiquarian questions and promoted the collaborative study of antiquity, exchanging views and materials not only within England but also with the Continent. The Society was also part of Cotton's network that helped him to acquire manuscripts containing OE. The register of his lenders (now BL, Harley 6018) illustrates Cotton's willingness to treat his collection as a working library.[55] In return, Cotton and his heirs benefited from a remarkable number of gifts and bequests from other owners, collectors and beneficiaries such as John Joscelyn, William Lambarde, Laurence Nowell, the antiquarian William L'Isle (1569?–1637), the astronomers and mathematicians John Dee and Thomas Allen (c. 1542–1631), as well as James Ussher (1581–1656), archbishop of Armagh. Despite this support from benefactors, the Cotton Library had a chequered history. Its closure in 1629 undoubtedly had a negative effect on its broad use, and the disastrous fires of 1731 (in the

---

[52] Known best by their sigla A–G. Lutz, 'Das Studium'.   [53] See p. 49.

[54] Wright, 'The Dispersal of Libraries'; Sharpe, *Sir Robert Cotton*, 49–51; Niles, *The Idea*, 88–91.

[55] Listed by Ker, *Catalogue*, lv. The full extent of damage to the OE holdings in the Cottonian collection can be observed from Wanley, *Catalogus*, and Smith, *Catalogus librorum*, both of which date from before the fire.

Cotton Library) and 1865 (in the British Museum bindery) damaged and destroyed some of its most prized items.[56] Neil Ker, while acknowledging that 'Cotton acquired considerably more manuscripts containing Anglo-Saxon than even Parker ever had', is scathing about Cotton's rebinding of manuscripts and reassigning of booklets.[57] Nonetheless, Cotton's practice of collection formed a move towards a national collection, of which his manuscripts of OE are a quintessential part.[58]

Unlike Cotton, Sir Thomas Bodley (1545–1613), whose name graces the library of Oxford University, never possessed any OE manuscripts himself. After a long career as a diplomat, Bodley devoted all his energy in the last fifteen years of his life to the restoration of the 'public' library, ceaselessly working to increase its collection and status. The earliest acquisitions of OE manuscripts are those with 'Bodley' and 'Auctarium' in the press marks. These manuscripts originate from a highly disparate ownership, with the Dean and Chapter of Exeter Cathedral providing the most items (296, 307, 308, 315, 316). Sir Walter Cope and Sir Robert Cotton gave volumes of Ælfric's *Homilies* (309, 310), while the money of Herbert Westphaling, bishop of Hereford, bought a manuscript of the OE Gospels (312). Among the twenty manuscripts donated by Thomas Allen, there is the miscellany known as 'St Dunstan's Class Book' (297), while Thomas Draper gave a manuscript of the OE Boethius (305). With this early influx of books, the tone had been set, and in the 17th century, the Bodleian Library's holdings of OE manuscripts grew mainly through the important bequests of Sir Kenelm Digby (319–21), Sir Christopher Hatton (324–33), Franciscus Junius (334–8), whose bequest included the Junius manuscript of OE poetry, and William Laud (342–6), to be followed in the 18th century by those of Richard Rawlinson (348–50) and Thomas Tanner, the bishop of St Asaph, who donated the 'Tanner Bede' (351).[59] Despite Bodley's efforts and the generosity of many benefactors, the Bodleian Library was, in the 17th century, no longer in a position to build up a collection of OE manuscripts comparable to that of Matthew Parker or Sir Robert Cotton. The same applies to the Royal Library, which holds twenty-six manuscripts containing OE (245–70), nine of which derive from a bequest by John, Baron Lumley (c. 1533–1609). By the 18th century, manuscripts of OE had attained a value and status not enjoyed since the early Middle Ages and were becoming luxury items in the collections of the super-rich, such as Robert Harley (1661–1724), the 'collector' Earl of Oxford, who was able to scramble together twenty manuscripts of OE (225–44) in the last major collecting effort.

---

[56] Prescott, 'Their Present Miserable State', 419–21.　　[57] Ker, *Catalogue*, liv–lv.

[58] See Wright, ed., *Sir Robert Cotton as Collector*, for a complete overview of Cotton's collecting activities.

[59] Ker, *Catalogue*, 349–429.

Collection presumes a need or wish to make available manuscripts, texts and knowledge of the corpus. The first list of 'Libri Saxonica lingua conscripti', a title that suggests an inventory of OE manuscripts and texts, appears in BL, Cotton Nero C. iii, fol. 208, in the hand of John Joscelyn. Written between 1565 and January 1567, the list contains fifteen items: eight lives of English saints, Eadmer's *Historia novorum in Anglia* and six versions of the *Anglo-Saxon Chronicle*.[60] For the first nine items, Joscelyn only identifies the text and, if known, the author. For the chronicles, which he numbered 1–6, Joscelyn mentions the provenance, the current owner, and, if possible, the time span covered by the text: it is clear that manuscripts are meant here. Although the title of the list refers to *Libri* 'books' written in OE, not all texts are in OE, and Joscelyn presumably intended to list sources for Anglo-Saxon history, rather than texts in OE.[61]

Texts in OE were definitely the focus of an inventory of *Monumenta Anglo-Saxonica* compiled by the Dutch philologist Franciscus Junius (1591–1677) for his *Gothicum Glossarium* (1665): an etymological glossary of Gothic vocabulary, explained with the help of lexical and textual material from other Old Germanic languages (see Figure 3).[62] OE was the language Junius

Figure 3 Franciscus Junius (from Rawlinson, *A. Manl. Sever. Boethii Consolationis Philosophiæ*)

---

[60] Edited by Graham and Watson, *The Recovery*, 55–9.
[61] Graham and Watson, *The Recovery*, 5–7. [62] Junius, *Gothicum glossarium*, ***2–***4.

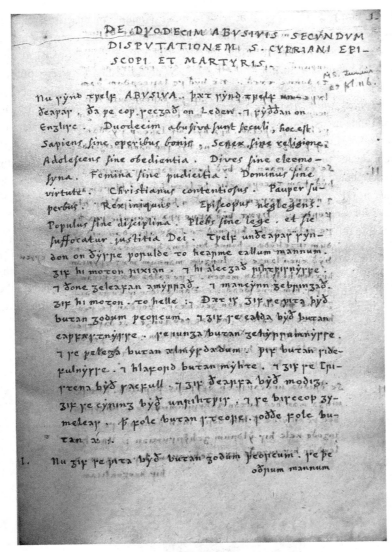

Figure 4 Oxford, Bodleian Library, Junius 48, f. 1r

studied most intensively, and collection was a prime aspect of his work. Between circa 1645 and circa 1670 he made some seventy-five transcripts of OE texts (see Figure 4) which he deemed useful for his etymological glossaries and for his *Lexicon Saxonicum* (OBL, Junius 2 and 3). The *Monumenta Anglo-Saxonica* is based on these transcripts, on OE texts printed before 1665 and on the OE manuscripts he possessed. Junius's focus is on texts, authors and translators, with provenance irregularly and incompletely indicated.

Important authors get a separate entry. Of Ælfric, Junius mentions *De veteri ac novo testamento*, as printed by William L'Isle in 1623, as well as the *Glossary*, *Grammar* and *Canones*,[63] but he leaves homilies and saints' lives unmentioned, while Ælfric's *De temporibus* is not attributed to him. The OE *Interrogationes Sigeuulfi in Genesin* are attributed to Alcuin. King Alfred, praised by Junius for his qualities as a ruler and for his appreciation of scholarship, is presented as the translator of Bede's *Historia ecclesiastica*, Pope Gregory's *Regula Pastoralis*, Boethius's *De consolatione*, Orosius's *Historiae adversum paganos* and Augustine's *Soliloquies*. Furthermore, Junius mentions the West Saxon Gospels, the Lindisfarne and Rushworth Gospels, hymns with interlinear glosses, the psalter with interlinear glosses, the OE laws from Lambarde's *Archaionomia*, the OE *Martyrology*, the pseudo-Gospel of Nicodemus, the *Vindicta Salvatoris*, the *Liber Scintillarum*, the OE *Benedictine Rule*, herbals and medical texts, Pope Gregory's *Dialogues*, Wulfstan's *Sermo lupi ad Anglos*, as well as smaller texts such as prognostications and a range of glossaries. Junius's inventory may be regarded as a first, rudimentary attempt to outline a canon of OE literature, albeit with some remarkable hiatuses – the most striking one being *Beowulf*, which he must have seen when he inspected BL, Cotton Vitellius A. xv, but did not mention. Yet, despite its flaws, no earlier publication had presented the extraordinary variation of OE literature to the scholarly world in print, and the *Monumenta Anglo-Saxonica* must have been an eye-opener to Junius's contemporaries and successors, to whom the contents of medieval manuscripts were only partially known. Rarely mentioned nowadays, it was very influential to the school of Oxford Saxonists who followed in Junius's footsteps.

Junius's influence appears strongly in the work of the churchman and antiquary George Hickes (1642–1715), whose *Institutiones Grammaticæ* (1689) and *Thesaurus* (1703–5) were both the culmination of OE philology in the 16th and 17th centuries and the foundation for its later developments. As part of the *Institutiones*, Hickes published in 1689 a *Catalogus veterum librorum septentrionalium*: the first inventory of texts and books in OE and other Old Germanic languages that was titled 'catalogue'. Like Junius, Hickes divided his inventory into sections, beginning with Gothic, followed by OE, Old High German, Frisian and the Scandinavian languages, and listed medieval manuscripts as well as early modern transcripts and printed books. The section on OE is the biggest by far. A list of printed books, titled *Libri Anglo-Saxonici excusi*, is followed by a survey of manuscripts and texts in

---

[63] Ælfric's letter to Bishop Wulfsige. Lambarde, *Archaionomia*, ed. Wheelock, 127–35.

Oxford libraries (pp. 135–50), with nine pages dedicated to the collection that Junius had donated to the Bodleian library in 1677. The next subsection describes the Cambridge holdings (pp. 150–66) with ten pages dedicated to Parker's collection in the library of Corpus Christi College. The final twelve pages (pp. 166–77) contain information on texts and manuscripts from the Royal Library, the libraries of Lord Lauderdale, Rochester Cathedral, Worcester Cathedral and Lambeth Palace, as well as the Cottonian Library and Canterbury Cathedral Archives. The section of information on the Cottonian collection is remarkably short. This unevenness in the degree of detail is due to the difficult circumstances under which Hickes, a nonjuring clergyman and bishop, was compelled to work: he had not been able to visit the library of Corpus Christi College, Cambridge, and found the Cottonian library closed when he attempted to visit it. Hickes had, therefore, been forced to rely on catalogues and information sent to him by well-wishers. Nonetheless, Hickes's library catalogues incorporates information from 120 medieval manuscripts, besides the printed editions and transcripts.[64]

The final great effort of collection in the early modern study of OE took place in the decades following the publication of Hickes's *Catalogus librorum septentrionalium*, and was partly indebted to it. In the middle of the 1690s, Hickes began to think of an expansion of his *Institutiones grammaticæ*, which he discussed with others, including his fellow bishop and antiquary William Nicolson (1655–1727), the OE and Greek scholar, Edward Thwaites (1661–1711) and Arthur Charlett (1655–1722), the Master of University College. It was through the agency of the latter that, in 1695, Hickes was put in touch with Humfrey Wanley (1672–1726), the son of a Coventry draper, an autodidact, and in due course, the founding father of OE palaeography and bibliographical scholarship. In his quest for learning, Wanley had copied by hand William Somner's *Dictionarium Saxonico-Latino-Anglicum*,[65] Hickes's *Grammatica Anglo-Saxonica et Moeso-Gothica* from the *Institutiones*, as well as the section on OE manuscripts from the *Catalogus librorum septentrionalium*, creating for himself a compendium of OE (now BL, Harley 3317).[66] Wanley's 'genius for understanding manuscripts in all their aspects', outstanding knowledge of alphabets and excellent memory were the main reasons why Hickes 'recruited' him to revise and complete the *Catalogus librorum septentrionalium*, a job which Wanley had finished by the spring of 1704.[67] The final product, amounting to a third of Hickes's *Thesaurus*, and published with a separate date (1705), and often in a separate binding, was without a doubt the most important book in

---

[64] Gneuss, 'Der älteste Katalog', 99–100.   [65] See pp. 27–31.
[66] Gatch, 'Humfrey Wanley', 48; Niles, *The Idea*, 156–8.   [67] Harris, *A Chorus*, 63.

the study of OE, to date.[68] Its qualities were summed up by Neil Ker in his *Catalogue of Manuscripts Containing Anglo-Saxon* that finally superseded Wanley's in 1957: Wanley's 'opinion on any given matter will always be worth knowing. A new catalogue is needed chiefly because in the course of 250 years a vast amount of work has been done on the texts and manuscripts Wanley first described'. Ker adds to this praise by stating that 'less than a dozen manuscripts containing a considerable amount of OE have been found in English libraries since Wanley wrote', and by reminding us that Wanley wrote before the Cottonian fire of 1731.[69] While Ker set narrower chronological and diplomatic boundaries than Wanley (no early Middle English, no charters, no full recording of the Latin contents), it is fair to say that Wanley's catalogue of English document materials containing OE is well-nigh complete even by modern standards.

Wanley's innovations in the organisation of his *Catalogus* are striking, as is the degree of detail and erudition in his descriptions. For the first time, the inventory is one of manuscripts as well as texts, and the manuscripts are organised according to libraries and press marks. For each manuscript, text items are numbered by Roman numerals and linked to page or folio numbers, the latter with recto or verso indications (a or b). Texts are identified by rubrics, printed in uncials, or by means of titles assigned by Wanley, for example, *Nomina Regum West-Saxonum* (216), for a genealogy in BL, Cotton Tiberius B. v, or, more famous, the '*tractatus nobilissimus poeticè scriptus*', for *Beowulf* (218). Many texts are supplied with incipits and explicits, some of which are exceptionally long, as well as with bibliographical comments. These comments are particularly rich in the first part of the *Catalogus*, which describes manuscripts from Oxford where Wanley was resident. This part of the *Catalogus* (1–106) was printed in long lines and sometimes offers an apparatus of alternative readings at the bottom of the page. Although the introductory remarks to the manuscripts vary considerably, they present concise, scholarly observations. Thus, Wanley described OBL, Bodley 342 as a 'membrane codex in folio with letters of the highest quality written before the conquest of England which took place in 1066. In it, there are homilies which are partly or completely derived from the writings of the Latin Fathers, and which are linked to the course of the entire year...'.[70] It indicates that Wanley was able not only to make pertinent codicological observations but also to draw conclusions from them. Elsewhere Wanley refers to glosses, to usage by editors or to former medieval or early modern owners. The *Catalogus*, therefore, provided its readers with

---

[68] *Librorum veterum Septentrionalium, qui in Angliæ bibliothecis extant, nec non multorum veterum codicum Septentrionalium alibi extantium catalogus historico-criticus.*
[69] Ker, *Catalogue*, xiii–xiv. [70] Wanley, *Catalogus*, 1 (translated from Latin).

palaeographical, codicological, textual and bibliographical information, and taught the student of OE all that was known to date about the manuscripts and their contents. For modern readers, it is important to realise that Wanley's *Catalogus* was for most of its contemporary readership all they were ever going to see of manuscripts of OE, which were, by then, safely locked away in libraries and notoriously difficult to access. Not only its contents, but also its execution and design were meant to convey the importance of the material under discussion. Wanley succeeded in accomplishing what no-one had done before him: to collect evidence of the surviving manuscript corpus of OE in a single book.

3 Recording Old English

One of the main aims of OE studies, from its beginnings until today, is the organisation of its lexicon into a systematic compilation – in traditional terms, a dictionary. This process is generally known as 'lexicography'. In a modern linguistic framework, lexicography implies the provision of norms for standard use and refers to basic lexicographical practice such as the making of regular dictionaries, which serve language in performance by providing linguistic knowledge to the user.[71] In the context of early modern studies of OE, lexemes (units of lexical meaning) were recorded and listed to register the norms and usage in an earlier language phase without the constraints of modern lexicographical principles, and I therefore use the term 'recording' to describe early modern activities aimed at gathering and listing the OE lexicon. There is a wide variety in scope and purpose of early attempts at the recording of OE in the early modern age: short, fragmentary word-lists testify to the first selection and recording of lexemes, whereas more extensive dictionary projects aimed at recording comprehensively their meaning, and sometimes their usage. In addition, there are lists covering specific semantic domains such as proper names and place names, plant names or names of animals, legal terms or words with their etymologies. These early modern word-lists and dictionaries are, in the words of John Considine, not just 'mere recordings of words', but also evidence of how their compilers created and celebrated a connection with the past, with the aim of defining and establishing the identity of a group of speakers or a nation, an idea he defines as 'designing heritage'.[72] A constant factor in the designing of heritage is the search for *antiquitas*, meaning 'that which is ancient and therefore considered morally upright'. This was the common ground for all humanist scholarship, including the study of OE.

---

[71] Hüllen, *English Dictionaries*, 6.   [72] Considine, *Dictionaries*, 5–10.

The earliest attempts at the recording of OE during the early modern period rely strongly on manuscripts containing OE texts with an explicit relation to equivalent Latin source exemplars, such as the West Saxon Gospels or the OE Bede. Prominent among these manuscripts are those containing glosses or glossaries. Early medieval scribes inserted OE explanations or translations between the lines or in the margins in order to gloss words of many Latin texts, particularly canonical works such as the Rule of St Benedict, Psalms and Gospels. Such Latin words or phrases (known as lemmata) and their OE glosses (known as *interpretamenta*) were perfect starting points for the recording of the lexicon. Besides text glosses, medieval scribes had created 'glossaries', which existed in the shape of glosses collected from one or more texts (*glossae collectae*), as found in BL, Cotton Cleopatra A. iii or Harley 3376, and class glossaries: bilingual lists of semantically related items, such as names for birds, trees or buildings. In their attempts to learn OE, pioneers such as John Leland, Robert Talbot and Robert Recorde had chanced on manuscripts of Ælfric's *Grammar*, which was often followed by his bilingual class glossary. Its popularity can hardly be overestimated. According to R. E. Buckalew, the early modern transcripts of Ælfric's glossary outnumber the original manuscripts and collectively produce evidence for five manuscripts which are now lost.[73] Buckalew's inventory also makes clear that Ælfric's *Glossary* was the most frequently transcribed OE text and that it had the widest dispersal, with copies existing in England and on the Continent. Besides profiting from early medieval glosses and glossaries, early modern scholars also compiled glossaries of their own. The earliest existing OE word list is Robert Talbot's bilingual (Latin and OE) glossary on ff. 13rv in his notebook (CCCC 379). Of its thirty-two entries, twenty-four derive from Genesis, while eight were taken from the OE Orosius in BL, Cotton Tiberius B. i, another text that could be read with the help of its Latin equivalent. In five cases Talbot also provided English translations, thereby setting the tone for future lexicographical efforts.[74]

The earliest recording activities also include OE place names. John Leland, for example, excerpted a long list of place names from BL, Cotton Tiberius B. i, no doubt with an eye to the history of English places which he had proposed to King Henry VIII in his *New Yeare's Gift*.[75] In her discussion of the relation between the recovery of OE and topography in the 16th century Rebecca Brackmann explains that Leland's penchant for place names was found not only in this list but also in his publications and that Laurence Nowell and William Lambarde were both familiar with Leland's work. William

[73] Buckalew, 'Leland's Transcript', 153–4.
[74] Graham, 'Early Modern Users', 279–82; Graham, 'The Earliest Old English Word List'.
[75] Graham, 'Anglo-Saxon Studies', 416.

Lambarde, the younger of the two, drew up a *Dictionarium Angliæ topogra-*
phicum et historicum, which was left unfinished and unpublished, only finding
its way to the press in 1730. For many of its lemmata Lambarde depended on
Laurence Nowell's index of place names in his heavily annotated copy of
Richard Howlet's *Abcedarium Anglico-Latinum*, an alphabetical Latin–
English school vocabulary (London, 1552), in which Nowell added thousands
of OE lexemes to the Modern English lemmata. In her analysis of the collabor-
ation between Nowell and Lambarde, Brackmann demonstrates that each place
name they recovered and plotted on maps in printed books and manuscripts
contributed to the restoration of English heritage.[76]

The concept of heritage also played a seminal role in the compilation of the
earliest general glossaries of OE.[77] The first was Laurence Nowell's
Vocabularium Saxonicum, one of his unfinished projects which he left with
William Lambarde before his departure for the Continent in 1567. The
Vocabularium Saxonicum is a personal document revealing what Nowell considered interesting about OE and which sources he used. Unlike many other
glossaries at the time, most interpretations are in Modern English – some even
in Nowell's native Lancashire dialect; only a minority are in Latin. Although the
Vocabularium was arranged formally in alphabetical order of the first three
letters, the ordering also follows semantic leads: for example, the entry for OE
'*dwelan* to seduce, to bring into errour. Item to erre. *Dwelan fram Godes*
geleafan' is followed shortly after by *gedwola, gedwolman, dwolian* and
gedwyld, a series of related lexemes falling within the semantic concept of
heresy. Whereas the manuscript of the *Vocabularium Saxonicum* was consulted
by many later lexicographers, it was, apparently, never meant to be printed.[78]
Instead, the first printed glossary of some 685 OE lexemes with Modern English
interpretations can be found in Richard Rowlands Verstegan's *A Restitution of*
Decayed Intelligence, a history of the English language produced in Antwerp in
1605. Like Nowell's *Vocabularium Saxonicum*, Verstegan's glossary is
a personal selection of lexemes with a variety of interpretamenta ranging
from simple translations to encyclopaedic information.[79] However, in
Verstegan's case, the history of England reflected in his glossary and language
studies is not insular and Protestant but Germanic and latently Catholic.[80]
Verstegan was undoubtedly keen to prove that the English heritage was linked

---

[76] Brackmann, *The Elizabethan Invention*, 87–147.

[77] See Lancashire, *Lexicon*, for entries on some of the dictionaries and glossaries discussed in this section.

[78] See Marckwardt, *Laurence Nowell's Vocabularium Saxonicum*, 18, 59; compare Brackmann, *The Elizabethan Invention*, 17.

[79] See Goepp, 'Verstegan's "Most Ancient Words"', and Considine, *Dictionaries*, 188–91.

[80] Hamilton, 'Richard Verstegan's *A Restitution*', 14–28; Niles, *The Idea*, 79–88.

to migration from the Continent and that English was part of a Germanic language family. By selecting for his lemmata many OE lexemes that were cognate with Dutch, Verstegan implicitly created a linguistic connection which matched the argumentation in the rest of *A Restitution*. Verstegan's glossary is, therefore, an integral part of his book and a statement about the Germanic origin of English.

A more comprehensive and general aim to record the OE lexicon emerges in the lexicographical work of John Joscelyn, whom Graham characterises as 'the outstanding sixteenth-century pioneer of OE lexicography'.[81] Inspired in all likelihood by Parker's wish for an OE 'Lexicon for the publick Benefit', Joscelyn set about collecting a store of OE vocabulary not long after he entered Parker's household in 1559.[82] The traces Joscelyn left in manuscripts and the surviving documents in his own hand, and in that of his most important collaborator John Parker, reflect a systematic search for vocabulary in places (manuscripts) where no-one had trodden before. Joscelyn's method has been reconstructed by Graham. As a first stage he underlined and glossed words in manuscripts, or wrote numbers over the words he selected in a particular text. Many of the words he picked must have been entered on notepapers, most of which have not survived. Joscelyn then re-arranged his entries into alphabetical glossaries, a series of which have been preserved in London, Lambeth Palace 692. Most pages in Lambeth 692 contain entries from a single manuscript in alphabetical order by the first letter only. Two non-alphabetical lists may contain extracts directly from manuscripts.[83] As the next stage, the entries from these alphabetical glossaries were entered in what is now known as Joscelyn's *Dictionarium Saxonico-Latinum* (BL, Cotton Titus A. xv and xvi), two substantial volumes, written partly by Joscelyn but mostly by John Parker, in which around 23,000 entries were added in alphabetical order of the first three letters (see Figure 5). The final stage of Joscelyn's work are the corrections and additions to the original entries, partly written in the space between entries and partly on additional sheets, one of which has survived as BL, Harley 6841, fol. 131.[84]

Joscelyn's 'ur-dictionary' of OE is a work that still raises many questions. Ever since John Strype's biography of Archbishop Parker, it has been surmised that Joscelyn's two volumes were essentially the outcome of his lexicography project and might have been used to typeset the first dictionary of OE.[85] At the same time, it has been repeatedly stressed that the contents of Joscelyn's *Dictionarium Saxonicum* are far from stable. Ruled for a limited number of

---

[81] Graham, 'John Joscelyn', 133; see also Hetherington, *The Beginnings*, 25–51.
[82] Graham, 'John Joscelyn', 94.   [83] *Ibid.* 104–27.   [84] *Ibid.* 127–32.   [85] *Ibid.* 94–6.

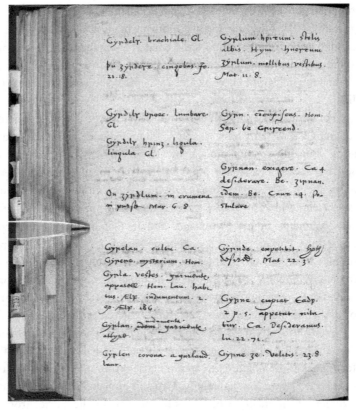

Figure 5 London, British Library, Cotton Titus A. xv, f. 220v

entries per page, the layout allows enough space for further additions, of which there are more at the beginning of the *Dictionarium* and fewer towards the end. Blank spaces suggest a work in progress with more entries to be added, but on what basis is unclear. The entries consist of OE lexemes followed by Latin translations and, irregularly, English translations, many of which derive from Nowell's *Vocabularium Saxonicum*. Morphological variants of the same lexeme often occur as separate entries. As a major innovation, most entries conclude with abbreviated source references, for example, '*Cicenu*. Pullos. chickens. Matt. 23.27. Ælf.'[86] Some of those guided the reader with relative ease to either manuscript sources, mentioning work or author, or to printed versions of OE texts available to Joscelyn, such as the Laws or Gospels. But many others are very personal or imprecise: for example, *hom* for homily, *hym* for hymns, or *lib*.

---

[86] Hetherington, *The Beginnings*, 183–5, lists references, many of which have meanwhile been identified by Graham.

tit., an unclear reference. Not infrequently, the source reference *Laur.* points to Laurence Nowell whose *Vocabularium Saxonicum* Joscelyn used, besides other materials from Nowell which no longer exist.[87] Although Parker's death in 1575 may have cut publication short, Joscelyn's plans were also thwarted by his ambitions. It is likely that Joscelyn was aiming for an OE–Latin–English dictionary, like the one William Somner produced almost a century later. Many English translations still had to be added, however. Moreover, the system of source referencing used by Joscelyn would have required an *apparatus* that was not in place. Even if one made allowances for the repetition of entries with morphological rather than lexical variants, the amount of work that needed to be done before a dictionary could be typeset and printed was so substantial that it might have required another handwritten version.

With the deaths of Matthew Parker, in 1575, and Joscelyn in 1603, the study of OE had lost its coordinator and its most prominent practitioner, but the seeds had been sown and attempts at recording the lexicon continued. A new generation of scholars approached the language in a new setting: many manuscripts had moved into more or less accessible collections; several texts were available in printed editions; individual antiquarian interests were slowly replacing the Elizabethan focus on religious and social Anglicanism; and the interest in OE increasingly branched out from England to the Continent. A number of what Hetherington calls 'smaller glossaries' were intended as exercises or personal compendia and formed part of the process of learning OE.[88] The easiest points of access to OE were the West Saxon Gospels, published in 1571; a glossary of OE vocabulary from these Gospels by Sir William Boswell (d. 1650), the English Ambassador in The Hague, is testimony to their use.[89] An anonymous document from around 1600, preserved in OBL, James 42, contains a rudimentary alphabetical list of OE lemmata and mostly Latin interpretamenta, followed by the words for numerals, a list of lexemes from the Gospels, a short class glossary, a list of 'olde woords' from Spenser's *Shepheardes Calender* and a list of rhyming monosyllables and suffixes. This is not a *Dictionarium Saxonico-Latinum*, as Thomas Hearne (*bap.* 1678–1735) titled it in the 18th century; instead, it is a workbook recording someone's first explorations into OE.[90] Other glossaries which were not intended for publication include the ones made by Richard James, Sir Robert Cotton's librarian.[91]

---

[87] Graham, 'John Joscelyn', 106–7.   [88] Hetherington, *The Beginnings*, 68–76.
[89] *Ibid.* 68. See also Bankert, 'Oxford, Bodleian Library, MS Rawlinson C.887', for the unpublished glossary compiled by Nathaniel Spinckes (1654–1727), which is based on printed editions only, and therefore evidence of Spinckes's reading list.
[90] Hetherington, *The Beginnings*, 69–71; Bennett, *The History*, 355.
[91] Hetherington, *The Beginnings*, 71–6; Bennett, *The History*, 355.

Besides these small-scale lexicographical exercises, of which there must have been more than were eventually preserved, at least ten other dictionary projects are known to have been undertaken or started in the period before 1659. Two of these were published, while four remain in manuscript form and four are lost:

1. An untitled dictionary by the judge and antiquary Francis Tate (1560–1616), compiled presumably towards the end of the 16th century. Now lost.[92]

2. A *Glossarium Anglo-Saxonico-Latinum* by the Hamburg lawyer and philologist Friedrich Lindenbrog (1573–1648), which contained an abridged version of John Joscelyn's *Dictionarium*, copied during a visit to London between 1614 and 1616 and supplemented with further minor glossaries.[93] Now Hamburg, Staats- und Universitätsbibliothek, Cod. germ. 22, pp. 1–325.[94] In northern Germany, at least three handwritten copies were made of Friedrich Lindenbrog's transcript of Joscelyn's *Dictionarium*: one by the historian and linguist Johann Georg von Eckhart (1664–1730), one by the philologist Dietrich von Stade (1637–1718) and one by Abraham Hinckelmann (1652–95) in the latter decades of the 17th century.[95]

3. An untitled dictionary by the philologist scholar William L'Isle, compiled around 1630. Now lost.[96]

4. An untitled dictionary by the Tally-Office clerk John Bradshaw, compiled presumably before 1631. Now lost.[97]

5. A *Dictionarium Citeriorum Sæculorum Anglo-Saxonicum-Latinum* … by the diarist and antiquary Sir Simonds D'Ewes (1602–50), which he worked on from 1626 to 1650. Now BL, Harley 8–9.[98]

6. A *Lexicon Saxonicum* by the Cambridge Arabist and OE scholar Abraham Wheelock (1593–1653), begun around 1638. Now BL, Harley 761.[99]

7. A book of *Verba Saxonica* by the antiquary and herald Sir William Dugdale (1605–86), begun around 1644. Now OBL, Dugdale 29.[100]

8. A *Lexicon Anglo-Saxonicum* by the Dutch theologian and polymath Johannes de Laet (1582–1649), begun around 1638. Now lost.[101]

---

[92] Hetherington, *The Beginnings*, 68–9; Bennett, *The History*, 354.

[93] Hetherington, *The Beginnings*, 77–9.

[94] On the rediscovery of this manuscript, see Rudolf and Pelle, 'Friedrich Lindenbrog's Old English Glossaries'.

[95] Rudolf, 'Old English Lexicography', 12–15.

[96] Hetherington, *The Beginnings*, 67–8; Bennett, *The History*, 355.

[97] Hetherington, *The Beginnings*, 117, 119.

[98] Hetherington, *The Beginnings*, 102–24; Bennett, *The History*, 359–60.

[99] Hetherington, *The Beginnings*, 80–6; Bennett, *The History*, 356–7.

[100] Hetherington, *The Beginnings*, 88–97; Bennett, *The History*, 360.

[101] Hetherington, *The Beginnings*, 97–102; Bennett, *The History*, 357–8; Bremmer, 'Mine Is Bigger than Yours', 144–61. See also Bremmer, 'The Correspondence', 161–2, on the remarkable circumstances of its loss.

9. The *Dictionarium Saxonico-Latino-Anglicum* by the antiquary William Somner (1598–1669), begun around 1650. It was printed in Oxford in 1659; the manuscript is Canterbury, Cathedral Archives, LitMS E20–1. An abbreviated and revised version titled *Vocabularium Anglo-Saxonicum*, compiled largely by Edward Thwaites, was published by Thomas Benson (Oxford, 1701).[102]

10. A *Lexicon Saxonicum* by Franciscus Junius, begun around 1645. It is now OBL, Junius 2, 3; an edited copy of it exists in BL, Add. 4720–2. Junius's *Lexicon Saxonicum* was the main source for the *Dictionarium Saxonico et Gothico-Latinum* published by Edward Lye and Owen Manning in 1772.[103]

The frequent attempts at recording OE during the 17th century should be seen in the light of two enabling factors. The first concerns the Parker circle's activities in the 16th century, as a result of which the OE Gospels and the laws were made available in print, the first attempt at recording OE had been made and the status of OE had improved. The second factor involves the foundation of a lectureship in OE at Cambridge by the historian and antiquary Sir Henry Spelman (1563/4–1641). The priorities for this new lectureship were the publication of historical resources, the preparation of an OE grammar and of an OE dictionary.[104] Besides the influence of Parker's inheritance and Spelman's sponsorship, the dictionaries themselves suggest that the motivations to study OE were becoming more diverse, indicating a changing philological and cultural focus. Four issues play particularly important roles in this changing field: the increasing availability of sources, the rising importance of the vernacular, the burgeoning interest in comparative philology and the change from producer-focused dictionaries to user-focused dictionaries.

The use of sources by the earliest generations of lexicographers has attracted substantial scholarly attention, and it is fair to say that each dictionary project differed in its compilation and referencing. Most conservative, perhaps, is Friedrich Lindenbrog's abridged and edited transcript of Joscelyn's work, to which no entries from other sources were added, even though Lindenbrog could have integrated other smaller OE glossaries he had copied.[105] All sources were therefore Joscelyn's, and to Lindenbrog's German readers, many of those would have made little sense. Like Lindenbrog, Sir Simonds D'Ewes also based his dictionary project on Joscelyn's *Dictionarium*, transcribed for him by an amanuensis. However, unlike Lindenbrog's *Glossarium*, which remained

---

[102] Hetherington, *The Beginnings*, 125–82; Bennett, *The History*, 361–2.
[103] Referred to by Hetherington, *The Beginnings*, 231–2; Bennett, *The History*, 363–8.
[104] Lutz, 'The Study', 35; Clement, 'The Beginnings of Printing', 242–3.
[105] Rudolf and Pelle, 'Friedrich Lindenbrog's Old English Glossaries', 619–626.

untouched after it had been copied, D'Ewes added material from other sources, including Ælfric's *Grammar*, and mobilised his scholarly network (Dugdale, Junius and Somner) to help him with additions from their own lexicographical studies.[106] D'Ewes's work, in turn, differed from that of Dugdale and Wheelock, both of whom did not start out from Joscelyn's *Dictionarium*, but compiled new collections of entries from both printed and manuscript sources. Source referencing remained problematic, however: whereas Wheelock dutifully referenced them all, Dugdale did so inconsistently.[107] This sample comparison highlights the complexity and, in particular, the methodological inconsistency in early dictionaries of OE: references are often opaque and serve the producer more than the user.

Similarly inconsistent is the introduction of the vernacular (Modern English) in dictionaries of OE. The period between 1550 and 1650 witnessed an increasing status for the vernacular in England, which added to the heritage value of OE. The wish to make the connection between Modern English and OE prompted Laurence Nowell and Richard Verstegan to use English interpretamenta in the *Vocabularium Saxonicum* and the glossary to the *Restitution of Decayed Intelligence*, and it may even have motivated Joscelyn and John Parker to add more English interpretamenta than the ones they had copied from Nowell. Remarkably enough, it was the antiquarian William Dugdale who compiled a dictionary of OE lemmata with Modern English translations throughout, instead of Latin ones. While Considine attributes Dugdale's choice to Sir Simonds D'Ewes's original plan to compile a 'Saxon dictionarie with the Latine & Modern English added to it',[108] it is the omission of Latin as the prime target language that is truly innovative. Dugdale foregrounds the relation between OE and Modern English, showing a primary interest in language rather than sources. This interest is also apparent from his attention to spelling variants of the same words, which he brackets in order to distinguish orthographical variation from other distinctions. As Hetherington notes,[109] Dugdale's lexicon was at some point annotated by William Somner, whose choices for his own dictionary may well have benefited from Dugdale's pioneering work.[110]

The recording of OE in printed form was finally achieved in 1659 by William Somner's *Dictionarium Saxonico-Latino-Anglicum* (see Figure 6). While Somner's *Dictionarium* fulfilled the wish for a dictionary expressed by Matthew Parker almost a century earlier, it was indicative of a new phase in the history of OE studies, born out of new interests and stimulated by new questions

---

[106] Hetherington, *The Beginnings*, 102–4.

[107] *Ibid*. 82, 96, alludes to some use of Joscelyn's dictionary, but the latter does not seem to have formed the basis.

[108] Considine, *Dictionaries*, 193.   [109] Hetherington, *The Beginnings*, 94.

[110] Fletcher, 'Most Active and Effectual Assistance', on his cooperation with William Dugdale.

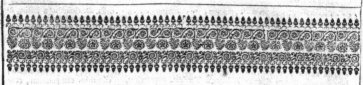

DICTIONARIUM
SAXONICO-LATINO-ANGLICUM.

| A | A B | A B |

Augmentum initiale, nonnunquam otio-sum, eóque per a-phæresin *Anglis* usi-tatissimam hodie sæ-pe præcisum. *E. G.* abæpan, to beate: abeoban, to bið: abpecan, to bpeake, & alia sexcenta. Atqui hoc ip-sum ex usu & genio linguæ Græcæ ad *Anglos* derivatum. quod, inter alia plura haud vulgaria, me docuit Studiorum mecrum fautor ille unicus, D. *Mericus Casaubonus*, magni quidem patris non minor fili-us, ac de me, & omnibus istius linguæ studiosis vir optime meritus,in laudatissimo de qua-tuor linguis tractatu, pag. 235. Particulam hanc *Alexander Gillius*, in *Logonom. Angl.* c. 9. vocat *epitaticam*: ut in a-mate. *i. terreo*; aber, *vehemen-tius affirmo pro vero*, &c.

A. (*ut be*, pop, ʒe, & to) ver-borum præteritis, præteriti temporis participiis, ac verba-libus, sæpe præpositum : cujus in sequentibus exemplorum sa-tis. Hic interim monendum, præpositiones hu jusmodi sæpe commutari.Quæ hic igitur de-siderantur, illic (in vocibus scil. à cæterarum unâ aut alte-râ incipientibus) nonnunquam inveniantur.

A. Semper, usque. Alwaies, e-ber. he bið à ymbe þ an. o-perose hoc unum melitur semper. item. in ævum, in æternum, in perpetuum, in seculum: foʒ e-ber, foʒ ap. à butan enð. *i. semper, absque fine.* à to po-pulbe.*in seculum.*

AA. idem. áà ʒý Gobeʒ nama ecclice ʒebletʒoð. *Collaude-tur nomen Dei in æternum.* ʒ uton bón. rpa uʒ Seapr ir. helpan áá ðam paðoʒt ðe

helpeʒ beʒt behopaþ. *Nos ve-rò* (*ut quidem par est*) *ut quisque maximè opis indigeat,ita ei sem-per potissimùm opitulemur.* Hoc linguâ Danicâ vetere, *æ.* V. *Worm: Literaturæ Runicæ* c. 27. p. 160.

Äac. quercus, robur. an **Dake.** linguâ Danicâ vetere eik. *Wor-mius. Kiliano*, eycke, &c. V. ac.

Äað. Congeries, strues, pyra, ligni congeries, rogus. a **Pile,** a **Wood-pile.** *Bed.* Hist.li. 3. c. 16.

Äalʒepep. Igniarium. a **Fire-steel:** also, **Tinder.**

Äam. Cauter. a **Searing iron.**

A B

Äbacen. Coctus, pistus. **Baked, oʒ baken.**

Äbæpan. Pati, tolerare to **bear, suffer,inðure.** *it.* ut abepan.

Äbal. Solertia, ingenium, scien-tia. **Cunning, Wit, Wisdome, knowledge, subtilty.** *it.* habi-litas. aptnesse, ability, able-nesse. —— heʒ þ þu pirreʒ opʒceʒ æce, cpæð þ þin a-bal ʒcpæʒc. ʒ þin moð-repa mapa punbe. ʒ þin lichoma leohtʒie micle. Diaboli A-damum tentantis verba sunt, *Parapb. Saxon.* pag. 25. *i. e. Præcepit* [Deus] *ut fructum hunc tu comedas:* dixit [mihi] *scientiam & peritiam tuam, mentisque tuæ intellectum* [inde] *auctum iri, & corpus tuum mul-to luculentius futurum.*

Äbannan. Mandare, præcipere, jubere, to **command.** *P. S.* p. 194. aban ðu þa beopnaʒ. bneʒo Calbea, ut oʒ orne. *Præcipe tu*, *Caldæorum Impe-rator*, [Nabuchodonosor] *vi-ris illis nobilibus*, [tribus pue-ris sc.] *ut de fornace exeant.* it:

edicere, denuntiare, proclama-re, publicare. to **publish**, to **proclaime.** ut abannan. e-dicto convocare, congregare, evocare. to **call foʒth**, sum-mon, congregate, oʒ call to-gether. *Teutonicis* eâdem sig-nificatione, & ab eodem fonte, bannen: barbarè, *bannire.* Hinc etiam nostratium bannes, pro nuptiarum pacto publica-to. Huc insuper (quod ad o-riginem attinet) referendum Gallorum *bannir*, Italorum *bandire*, nostratium bannish. *i.* proscribere, in exilium agere; & inde derivata: sed & nostra-tium **banning:** *i.* diræ, sinistra imprecatio, execratio. Videat hîc qui velit Cl. Equitis *Spel-manni*, & doctiss. *Vossii* Gloss. in voce *bannum.it.Menagii* Les Origines de la Langue Fran-coise, in *ban.*

Äbapian. Denudare, prodere, o-stendere, manifestare. to **make bare, to betʒay, to detect,** to **disclose, to discover**, to **de-clare oʒ make manifest.** *Teu-ton.* eodem sensu baeren. *Ki-lian.*

Äbbað, Abbas. an **Abbat.**

Äbban-bune. *Abindoniæ* oppi-dum in agro *Berceriensi.* **Ab-bingdon**, *al.* Abbington, in **Barkshire.** ab Abbatiâ sic di-ctum, q.d. Abbatiæ mons, vel collis: olim autem (Cl. *Camb-deno* teste) **Sheoverham :** de quo loco, ex vetusto libro Ab-bendonensi, hæc (inter alia) idem commemorat *Cambde-nus: Hic sedes regia, huc cùm de regni præcipuis & arduis tractaretur negotiis concursus fiebat populi.* Hæc autem loco illi ad concilia annuatim cele-branda ab Anglo-Saxonibus designato, venerabili Bed e **Cloveshooh**, aliis **Clovesho,** quibusdam

A

Figure 6 Somner, *Dictionarium Saxonico-Latino-Anglicum,* A1r

and insights. On the one hand, as has been argued widely, Somner was a grateful user of the work of his predecessors and friends, which he acknowledged in his letter to the reader.[111] Somner may, therefore, rightly be seen as a catalyst through which the work of Nowell, Joscelyn, Verstegan, D'Ewes and Dugdale entered a new phase of recording the OE lexicon. On the other hand, Somner's *Dictionarium* was no longer a catalogue of lexemes with source references inserted solely for the benefit of its compiler. Instead, it was a dictionary designed to meet the needs of its users – a new generation of users, students especially. Around 1650, Somner started work on the *Dictionarium*, for which he collected materials and transcribed texts requiring long-term study, including biblical poetry from what is now OBL, Junius 11.[112] Neatly spaced out in three columns per page, the OE lemmata in the *Dictionarium* are translated into Latin and English. The languages are distinguished by their fonts: a newly made set of Anglo-Saxon types for the OE; roman for Latin and a black letter for English and other vernacular languages. Standard entries are limited to translations, but a fair number of them contain additional information, including citations from the OE source texts and from additional sources providing etymological, contextual and historical information. Wishing to judge historical dictionaries by modern stand-ards, critics have classified Somner's *Dictionarium* as a mere glossary, inferior to earlier dictionaries on account of its sparsity of citations. Hetherington complains that the study of OE had ended up with 'a student's rather than a scholar's dictionary',[113] an anachronistic distinction and historical fallacy, since in those days there were no scholars of OE in the modern sense of the word.

For students, Somner's *Dictionarium* offered not just a glossary of OE lexemes and translations, but also a treasure trove of knowledge concerning OE phonology and morphology and culture. Numerous entries concern place names derived from Bede's *Historia Ecclesiastica* and the *Anglo-Saxon Chronicle*. Legal history can, for example, be seen in the entry for *Deaðes-scyldig* ('guilty of death'), in which he cites a clause from the treaty between Alfred and Guthrum about the conviction of clergymen; cultural history in the entries for *Dry* and *Dry-men* ('magician'), which he links to druids; etymology in the entry for *dwelian* ('to seduce'), which is linked to 'to dwell'; natural history in the names of plants and stones;[114] morphology in the number of combinations with the suffix *-dom* and in the entry for the noun suffix *-ling*.[115] Most remarkable is that Somner's *Dictionarium* was the first to present examples of poetic diction, in entries such as *gamolferhð* ('advanced in years') from *Genesis A*, *Ganotes-bæð* ('gannet's

---

[111] Somner, *Dictionarium*, a4r–b2r; Hetherington, *The Beginnings*, 149–56.

[112] Lutz, 'Zur Entstehungsgeschichte', 17–20.   [113] Hetherington, *The Beginnings*, 145.

[114] Somner, *Dictionarium*, I1r, I4rv, K1r; Fletcher, 'William Somner's *Dictionarium*', 48–50.

[115] *Ibid*. I2v–I3r, Bb1v; See also Brackmann, *Old English Scholarship*, 127–160.

bath', a kenning for 'sea') from *The Death of Edgar* and *hronrad* ('whale road', another kenning for 'sea') from *Genesis A*.[116] While Somner's *Dictionarium* offers a recording of OE, it can also be read as an encyclopaedia of Anglo-Saxon England, based on Somner's own antiquarian knowledge, his sources and the help of his friends and colleagues.

One of those friends and colleagues whom Somner mentions in his prefatory letter to the reader is Franciscus Junius, whose *Lexicon Saxonicum* (OBL, Junius 2 and 3) was compiled alongside Somner's *Dictionarium*. Consisting of two volumes of folders, each of which covers a letter of the alphabet, Junius's *Lexicon* is a reflection of his own OE studies, which he conducted from the middle of the 1640s until the end of his life. The different sizes of the leaves in the folders (the smallest ones are the oldest) indicate that his project was ever growing, and that it was meant to do so.[117] Over the years Junius kept on adding entries, which he arranged in such a way that there was space for insertions and additions. Using his own library of printed books and the numerous transcripts of OE texts which he made over the years, Junius collected attestations with clear references, for example, '*Blotan, Sacrificare; Oros.* II, 2. IV, 4 & 7. *Blotan, victimare; Pastoral.* XLV, 4. *Blotan, Immolare; Orosius* IV. 4', in many cases adding citations of substantial length.[118] The system was aimed at allowing Junius to map the various shades of meaning of a lexeme, with clear references to the texts from which the data originated.[119] At some stage after around 1655, Junius started adding Gothic and Old Norse entries to the OE ones: the Gothic lexemes, with Greek translations, were excerpted from the *Codex Argenteus*;[120] the Old Norse ones derived from the works of Danish antiquarian and natural historian Olaus Wormius (1588–1654). Effectively, the addition of these two extra languages converted the *Lexicon Saxonicum* into a *Lexicon trium linguarum*, listing side by side entries from what Junius considered to be three major Old Germanic languages.

Franciscus Junius's comparative approach inspired the major 18th-century attempts at the recording of OE. With the bequest of his manuscripts and annotated books to the Bodleian Library in 1677, Junius's numerous glossaries and transcripts became available to a wider scholarly audience.[121] At the same time, the acquisition of Junius's letter fonts, including types for OE, Gothic and Runic, by the newly founded Oxford University Press, incited its founder,

---

[116] *Ibid*. P2v, Y4v, Aa4r; Fletcher, 'William Somner's *Dictionarium*', 41–2.

[117] Dekker, 'That Most Elaborate One of Francis Junius', 306–8.   [118] OBL, Junius 2, 29v.

[119] Dekker, 'That Most Elaborate One of Francis Junius', 322–36.

[120] A 6th-century manuscript containing the Gospels in Gothic. Its rediscovery and identification in the middle of the 1560s inspired and informed the study of Old Germanic languages. In 1654 it came into the possession of Isaac Vossius (1618–1689), who entrusted it to Franciscus Junius, who transcribed, edited and published the text. It is now in Uppsala University Library.

[121] Stanley, 'The Sources', 159–60.

Bishop John Fell (1625–86), to initiate a printing project which was based on the *Lexicon Saxonicum*, with additional material from other glossaries. Ambitiously titled *Dictionarium Septentrionale sive Promptuarium vocum Anglo-Saxonicarum, Gothicarum, Francicarum, Runicarum et Islandicarum, Latinè et Anglicè redditarum*, this eleven-volume dictionary of northern languages, which also includes Old Frisian, was compiled by the clergyman and scholar William Nicolson (1655–1727), but remained unpublished.[122]

The Junius manuscripts also caught the attention of the clergyman and philologist Edward Lye (1694–1767), who was arguably the most important scholar of OE in the 18th century after Hickes and Wanley. Like Junius, Lye was gifted with a brilliant mind and dedicated his life to scholarship. Among his major projects we find his edition of OBL, Junius 4 and 5, Junius's etymological dictionary of the English language, titled *Etymologicum Anglicanum*, which Lye published with additions and emendations in 1743. Junius's etymologies contain not only a substantial number of supposed OE roots, but also citations intended to expose the semantic range of the lexemes he discussed. Using his phenomenal knowledge of languages, Lye added substantially to Junius's work, for example, by adding more OE roots to Modern English words in the *Etymologicum*,[123] for which he used the transcript of OBL, Junius 2 and 3, Junius's *Lexicon Anglo-Saxonicum*, which had been paid for by Edward Harley, the second Earl of Oxford.[124] Lye's use of these transcripts ultimately resulted in the publication of the *Dictionarium Saxonico- et Gothico-Latinum*, in 1772, some five years after he died. The final work and publication of Lye's dictionary was carried out by the clergyman and scholar Owen Manning (1721–1801), to whom Lye had left the manuscripts with the provision that Manning would complete the work. Manning's outstanding knowledge of OE enabled him not only to complete what Lye had left him, but to add significantly to the quantity and quality of the *Dictionarium*, which appeared in two volumes. Lye's *Dictionarium* which, as Clunies Ross and Collins remind us, has often been misrepresented and downplayed, was actually 'a considerable advance on all its predecessors' and 'the most considerable achievement of Anglo-Saxon Studies in the early Georgian era'.[125] Its extensive use of Somner's and Junius's dictionaries combined the best of both. Its inclusion of vocabulary from the Exeter Book, in addition to words from OBL, Junius 11, increased its volume of poetic diction and citations from verse. Its *Notarum explicatio* at the beginning

---

[122] OBL, Fell 8–18; Dekker, 'That Most Elaborate One of Francis Junius', 339–41; Niles, *The Idea*, 167–8.

[123] Clunies Ross and Collins, *The Correspondence*, 35–8.

[124] London, British Library, Add. 4720–2. Lye in Junius, *Etymologicum Anglicanum*, B1v.

[125] Clunies Ross and Collins, *The Correspondence*, 43–9, at 46; Bennett, *The History*, 192–8.

of volume I explained the source references to the reader. The most striking improvement, however, is its methodology and conciseness: most entries consist of the lemma, translation(s) and the source reference(s), for example '*gliw-beam*. Tympanum; Ps. 149.3'.[126] Citations are relatively sparse and are mostly limited to extracts from verse texts. Moreover, the type of encyclopaedic information offered by Somner is rare. For the first time, a dictionary of OE in the modern sense of the word saw the light.

Lye and Manning's *Dictonarium* concluded more than two centuries of attempts to record the OE language. The efforts invested in glossaries and dictionaries were remarkable and show the importance attached to the recording of vocabulary, not only in England but also on the Continent where humanist scholars regarded OE as a vital link in the chain of Germanic languages that defined a shared past. Glosses and glossaries figured widely in the exchange of materials between individual scholars who were linked through wide-ranging scholarly networks. An important node was the University of Leiden (founded 1575) where the famous humanists Joseph Justus Scaliger (1540–1609) and Bonaventura Vulcanius (1538–1614) were professors at the time when Friedrich Lindenbrog and Johan de Laet were students. The surviving correspondence from within these networks shows that there were contacts, for example, between Lindenbrog and the antiquarian William Camden (1551–1623); between Scaliger and Marcus Welser; and between Camden and Janus Gruter (1560–1627), the librarian of the Heidelberg Palatine Library. Like Lindenbrog, Gruter was a correspondent of the Heidelberg scholar Marquard Freher (1565–1614), who published the Decalogue, the Lord's Prayer and the Creed in OE.[127] Later in the 17th century both Johan de Laet and Franciscus Junius were spiders in webs of international scholarly correspondence that featured OE widely, and often focused on words and glossaries.[128] Less conspicuous, but not uncommon in the Low Countries were direct contacts, for example between de Laet and his Leiden colleague Marcus Zuerius Boxhorn (1612–53), who inherited the manuscript of de Laet's dictionary, or between Junius and the Dutch lawyer and philologist Jan van Vliet (1622–66), who also studied OE in a comparative and multilingual setting. Although continental scholars contributed to all aspects of OE scholarship during the early modern period, their participation in the recording of the lexicon stands out as considerable and inspiring. Their networks formed the beginning of OE studies as the international discipline which it is today.

---

[126] Lye and Manning, *Dictionarium*, Bbbb2r.

[127] Rudolf and Pelle, 'Friedrich Lindenbrog's Old English Glossaries', 618–21.

[128] Bremmer, 'The Correspondence'; Van Romburgh, '*For My Worthy Freind Mr Franciscus Junius*', passim.

4 Editing Old English

Today, nearly all OE texts that have survived the bibliographical losses incurred by time and circumstances have either been printed in full or have been incorporated in the apparatus of some printed edition. Many texts have been printed more than once, and new editions of OE texts have continued to appear. Anthologies and internet publications have added to the availability of OE texts in print or on the screen. However, this generous availability of printed OE texts is rather recent: relatively few OE texts, most of which were prose, appeared in print before the 19th century.[129] Moreover, before the publication of *A Testimonie of Antiquitie* on the initiative of Matthew Parker in 1566/7, there was no printed OE of any substance.[130] For the question of how to edit and how to print an OE text, Parker and his associates turned to the humanist conventions and precedents of scholarly editing and printing. Like Latin and Greek texts, OE texts originated in manuscripts, which were regarded as the imperfect products of scribes who not only made copying mistakes, but sometimes also failed to indicate where texts began or ended and provided no titles. Although the editors' knowledge of OE fell far short of what was known about Latin, the history of editing OE was, from its very beginnings, characterised by the humanist wish to improve the text. Readings could be subject to emendation on the basis of the charting of variants from different versions of the same text (known as *recensio*) and reconstruction on the basis of philological knowledge (known as *divinatio*). Despite these 'improvements', OE texts were printed in such a way that they resembled the manuscripts.

Printing OE was the final and perhaps most challenging part of the editorial process. Printing habitually involved typesetting, proof printing, proofreading and correcting the composition, before the actual printing – all done by hand – could take place. The first hurdle that needed to be taken before OE texts could be printed was the production of a suitable letter font. The original scribes had written OE texts in peculiarly shaped Insular minuscule letters (ð, ꝼ, ᵹ, ꞃ, ꞅ, ꞇ, ẏ) as well as several letters that were not part of the traditional Latin alphabet (þ, ð, ƿ), the tironian note ⁊ and the abbreviation þ for *þæt*. Many of the early modern students of OE – though not all – copied the texts imitating the original manuscript hands, rather than adapting familiar letter forms and transliterating the additional graphs. The reason for this copycat behaviour was their conviction that these letter forms were emblematic of OE,[131] in the way that, for example, ancient Latin texts were associated with Carolingian minuscule, referred to as *litera antiqua* and reproduced as 'Roman' fonts for printing. For

---

[129] Godden, 'Old English', 9–11.   [130] Kelemen, 'More Evidence', 373.
[131] Parkes, 'Archaizing Hands', 123. Clement 'The Beginnings of Printing', 206.

Figure 7 [Parker], *A Testimonie of Antiquitie*, 19v, 20r

Matthew Parker, it was imperative that the printed text of *A Testimonie of Antiquitie* reflected the singularities of OE vernacular minuscule in its printing types (see Figure 7). Defending his use of Insular letter forms in the printing the Latin text of *Ælfredi regis res gestæ* (1574), Parker claimed that their reading would restore to readers the memory of the old but once familiar language and supply no small apparatus of hidden knowledge.[132] The association of this graphematic reflection of the past with the perceived ancient doctrines of the English Church will have been Parker's main motivation to sponsor the production of puncheons with which such letters could be printed. The special Anglo-Saxon character types had to be produced in such a way that they could be used together with an existing font of 'Roman' letters. Letter forms had to be designed and then cut in negative (mirror) image into steel puncheons, a precision job that could be done only by the most skilled metal workers. The puncheons were then stamped into copper blocks to produce (positive) matrices, which could be used to cast (negative) letters, also known as sorts, made of a lead alloy, to produce a positive image on the paper. The process was time-consuming and expensive, which may have been the reasons why early continental editions of minor OE texts by Bonaventura Vulcanius and Marquard Freher used exclusively Roman letters for printing OE.[133] The history

---

[132] Lucas, 'Parker, Lambarde', 41; Niles, *The Idea*, 65–70.

[133] Vulcanius, *De literis*, 73–80; see p. 53. Freher, *Decalogi orationis symboli*, A2r–A4r. See the list of primary printed sources for the chronological sequence of editions.

of Anglo-Saxon types has been extensively researched by Richard Clement, who meticulously specifies all fonts up to around 1640,[134] and by Peter Lucas, who explains that Parker founded a tradition of printing OE with Anglo-Saxon types that lasted until the 19th century, with a brief recurrence in 1997.[135] The design of Parker's type face, produced for the publication of *A Testimonie of Antiquitie* and based predominantly on the hand of OBL, Junius 121, set the tone for the printing of OE texts in the 16th and early 17th centuries, after which other typefaces were designed from a wider variety of manuscript variants.[136] The one produced for Franciscus Junius was used, after his death, at the Oxford University Press, whose archive still holds most of the puncheons.[137]

With printing came proofreading, an aspect which is often overlooked in the study of editions and which was carried out either by professional correctors or by the editors themselves, depending on whether any of the staff in a printing house could read with some credibility the text that had come off the galley. In the case of OE texts, the chances of finding such a reader were very slight indeed, as a result of which we must assume that most editors of texts or authors of dictionaries read their own proofs before the final text could be produced. This implies an extraordinary commitment in time and effort on the part of editors, who might have to move house temporarily to be present at the production process: we know about Franciscus Junius that he moved into rented accommodation in Dordrecht between 1663 and 1665 to be present at the printing of the Gothic and OE Gospels and the ensuing glossaries, while closely collaborating with his friend and co-editor Thomas Marshall who also resided in Dordrecht.[138] Not surprisingly, printing OE texts during the early modern period (as any printing) came with considerable expenses and often with great financial worries. Lucas has calculated that Archbishop Parker may have paid as much as 200 pounds (the price of two 'medium-sized average motor car[s] with all the extras') for the creation of two sets of special sorts (i.e., puncheons) necessary for John Day's printing press to commence his OE publications. Punch cutters with the necessary skills and expertise could only be found outside of England, and Frenchmen such as Pierre Haultin, François Guyot or his son Gabriel have been named as Day's suppliers.[139] Parker's investment demonstrates, in Lucas's

---

[134] Clement, 'The Beginnings of Printing'.   [135] Lucas, 'A Testimonye', 147–88, at 181.

[136] Lucas, 'Abraham Wheelock', analyses Abraham Wheelock's use of manuscripts for his Anglo-Saxon type-designs.

[137] Van Romburgh, *'For My Worthy Freind Mr Franciscus Junius'*, 848–51.

[138] Van Romburgh, *For My Worthy Freind Mr Franciscus Junius'*, 1006, 1018.

[139] Lucas, 'A Testimonye', 167–9; Clement, 'The Beginning of Printing', 207.

words, 'a measure of his commitment', but at the same time such sponsorship divulges the depth of archiepiscopal coffers.[140] Many others were not so well off. Franciscus Junius invested a large part of his income earned over years as a tutor and librarian in the Earl of Arundel's household to pay for his fonts; the printing of George Hickes's *Thesaurus*, a process that took seven years, could only be completed at great personal expense: Hickes incurred a debt of £ 500 and ended up with 100 unsold copies.[141]

The practical difficulties concerning printing and financing (the two went hand-in-hand) must have contributed to the substantial number of aborted editing projects of which there is evidence. Thus William L'Isle produced transcripts of the OE psalter and a compilation of Old Testament material, including the OE *Pentateuch*, neither of which he published.[142] Edward Thwaites planned editions of the *Anglo-Saxon Chronicle*, the OE translation of Gregory's *Pastoral Care*, the *Lindisfarne and Rushworth Glosses* and the laws in Old English.[143] William Elstob (1674?–1715) published a specimen of an edition of the OE *Orosius*, and, like Thwaites, worked on an edition of the laws and Gregory's *Pastoral Care*.[144] David Wilkins reputedly planned to publish *Orosius* with William Elstob's materials,[145] and both George Hickes and Humfrey Wanley made plans to re-edit Junius's edition of biblical poems, with a translation and with the manuscript illustrations added.[146] It is interesting to see that some of these planned editions were eventually realised: in 1640, three years after L'Isle died, John Spelman published an edition of the OE psalter; Edward Thwaites published the OE Heptateuch in 1698, and the OE Orosius was published eventually, in 1773, by Daines Barrington. Yet others never materialised or hardly got off the ground. A new edition of the psalter by Elizabeth Elstob (1683–1756), who disapproved of Spelman's work, never went beyond the planning stage,[147] while only a set of proofs (thirty-six pages) was ever printed of her aborted edition of Ælfric's two series of *Catholic Homilies*, which she completely transcribed.[148]

Important benchmarks were set by the first two editions of OE texts, one of which appeared in print, and the other, surprisingly enough, in manuscript. While most studies of OE philology regard Matthew Parker's *A Testimonie of*

---

[140] Lucas, 'Parker, Lambarde', 44–5.

[141] Lucas, 'Junius, His Printers', 178–81; Harris, *A Chorus*, 106–7.

[142] Bennett, *The History*, 311–2.   [143] *Ibid.* 322.

[144] Bennett, *The History*, 322; see Graham, 'William Elstob's Planned Edition of the Anglo-Saxon Laws'; Niles, *The Idea*, 159.

[145] See Bennett, *The History*, 331, who bases this asumption on Hearne, *Collections*, IX, 342. Graham, 'William Elstob's Planned Edition of the Anglo-Saxon Laws', 294–5, shows that Elstob's transcript of Orosius was acquired by the antiquary Joseph Ames (1687–1759). Wilkins obtained Elstob's materials on the Old English Laws.

[146] Bennett, *The History*, 323, 329.   [147] *Ibid.* 326.   [148] Gretsch, 'Elizabeth Elstob', 176–9.

Antiqvitie as the first edition, Rebecca Brackmann and Carl Berkhout have pointed to BL, Henry Davis 59 as an attempt by Laurence Nowell to produce an edition and translation of the laws of King Alfred. Written on vellum, with the OE text in minuscule script and the translation in humanist cursive on facing pages, the book was made, in all likelihood for a patron, although it is unclear who that might have been. The blue, red, green and gold ink used for initials and names suggest an expensive gift. The translations are of high quality, and the OE text 'represents the results of Nowell's collation and copying' of all texts known to him, which led Carl Berkhout to classify this text as the 'first critical edition of the laws of Alfred'.[149] As part of his collating efforts, Nowell made transcripts from manuscripts of OE laws, such as BL, Cotton Otho B. xi, CCCC 383 and BL, Harley 55, but he also translated parts of the so-called *Quadripartitus*, an early 12th-century translation of the OE laws into Latin, back into OE. Rather than a critical edition, Nowell's text of King Alfred's law is therefore an eclectic one, based on a comparison of various versions.

Nowell's methodology heavily influenced the production and reception of the first printed edition of the laws in OE, the *Archaionomia* published in 1568 by William Lambarde, as Nowell passed on his papers and his knowledge to Lambarde before leaving for the Continent in 1567. While the exact nature of their cooperation may never be clear, Patrick Wormald has argued that Lambarde used Laurence Nowell's transcripts and OE translation of the *Quadripartitus*, in addition to one or more medieval manuscripts.[150] As a result, several of Lambarde's readings do not occur in any medieval manuscript: for example; the form *æþelborenran* ('more nobly born') in Lambarde's 'Gif æþelborenran wifmen ðis gelimpe' ('if this happens to more nobly born women') (Alfred 11.5) occurs in all manuscripts as *borenran*, which is a scribal error. The emended form *æþelborenran* was presumably constructed by Nowell on the basis of the expression *nobilius oriunda* ('born more nobly') in the *Quadripartitus*.[151] Such variant readings (Wormald lists 134 for the laws of Alfred-Ine only) caused Felix Liebermann, the early 20th-century editor of the laws, to speculate that Lambarde used manuscripts which no longer exist, a thesis that was swatted down by the Oxford scholar and publisher Kenneth Sisam, who attributed the variants to Nowell's translation of *Quadripartitus*.[152]

The result of Nowell's and Lambarde's work was an eclectic edition which did not faithfully reproduce any of the manuscripts of the OE laws. Instead, like

---

[149] Brackmann, 'Laurence Nowell's Edition'; Berkhout, 'Laurence Nowell', 3.

[150] Wormald, 'The Lambarde Problem'; see Bately, 'John Joscelyn', 435, fn. 2, for the manuscripts rendered by Nw1–5; Niles, *The Idea*, 62–5.

[151] Wormald, 'The Lambarde Problem', 26; Liebermann, *Die Gesetze*, I, 56–7.

[152] Sisam, 'The Authenticity', focuses on I Athelstan, but presents a clear picture of the dispute.

humanist editors of classical texts, they produced a version of which they will have assumed that it was closer to the original and freed from the corruptions introduced by copying scribes. This situation did not change much with Abraham Wheelock's expanded second edition of the *Archaionomia*, which came out in 1644 with editions and additions by Sir Roger Twysden (1597–1672). In 1721, yet another edition of the laws was published by the orientalist and librarian David Wilkins (1685–1745), who included material from the *Textus Roffensis* and made a new Latin translation. For most texts, however, the basis remained Lambarde's (and therewith Nowell's) edition, which caused Patrick Wormald to observe that 'editorially, however, this was not much of an improvement on Lambarde/Nowell', and that few of 'Lambarde's perversities' had been corrected.[153] Although Wormald's rather damning criticism is factually correct, it also betrays an attitude to early modern editorial scholarship that sets modern editions as the only benchmark. Historiographically, such an attitude carries the risk of being anachronistic. Rather than testing old editions against the new, we need to ascertain why editors adopted certain methods and how their methods changed over time, which were the questions that editors asked from their texts, and, most importantly, what their readers found important, and why. Only then can we understand the significance attached to OE texts at the time of their publication.

Not all early modern editors of OE texts adopted the method of Nowell and Lambarde; instead, the early modern editions of OE texts are characterised by a variety of editorial methods. The evidence surrounding the editing and printing of *A Testimonie of Antiquitie*, analysed meticulously by John Bromwich, Peter Lucas and Timothy Graham, reveals how manuscript owners, editors and printers worked in close cooperation. Published in 1566/7 with the aim of demonstrating that 'Anglo-Saxon' doctrines surrounding the Eucharist and transubstantiation confirmed those current in the Anglican church, *A Testimonie* was produced in all likelihood by John Joscelyn and has as its central text Ælfric's *Paschal Homily* (*Sermo de Sacrificio in die Pascae*). This text was printed initially from a transcript conflated from two manuscripts which were both in Parker's custody: CCCC 198 and BL, Cotton Faustina A. ix. Bromwich discovered evidence of two proofing stages: (1) a set of discarded printed leaves bound into CUL Ii.4.6 (another manuscript containing this homily) and (2) a preliminary version of *A Testimonie* (now BL, Add. 18160) with the handwritten signatures of Parker and the English bishops.[154] The first edition, ensuing from the second proofs (ESTC S124446) was once

---

[153] Wormald, *The Making*, 22, fn. 102; see also Brackmann, *Old English Scholarship*, 69–101.
[154] Bromwich, 'The First Book', 282–3; Niles, *The Idea*, 57–60.

more corrected and reprinted (ESTC S122220): this is the version that is now most common and that was reprinted in facsimile in 1970.[155] That the original manuscripts were used to correct the proofs is suggested by pencil marks in CCCC 198 and BL, Cotton Faustina A. ix.[156] Lucas and Graham have observed that for the other major texts in *A Testimonie*, Ælfric's pastoral letter for Wulfsige and Ælfric's second letter to Wulfstan, the original manuscripts, CCCC 190, pp. 305–6, and OBL, Junius 121, ff. 116 r–118 r, were also marked up by Parker's staff to facilitate editing and serve as exemplars at the proof-reading stage.[157]

A similar conflation of two manuscripts lay at the basis of the edition of the West Saxon Gospels, published by John Day, the same printer that produced *A Testimonie*. While the dedication to Queen Elizabeth boasts the auspicious name of John Foxe, the martyrologist, it has been generally acknowledged that Parker's staff, including Joscelyn, must have contributed the lion's share to this book.[158] Its purpose, as Foxe's preface clearly states, was in the first place to demonstrate that vernacular Bible translations had existed in early medieval England and that the Reformation constituted 'a reduction of the Church to the Pristine state of olde conformitie'.[159] A rudimentary examination by Walter Skeat in 1871 concludes that *The Gospels of the Fower Evangelistes* is 'a tolerably correct print of OBL, Bodley 441, with a few corrections from the Cambridge manuscript [CUL, Ii. 2. 11]'. In the process from script to print, as Skeat observed, the editors disregarded vowel accents, changed þ to ð in final position and frequently inserted y for i, inserted modern capitalisation, expanded contracted forms and made occasional emendations.[160] In the editorial process, Parker's team marked up OBL, Bodley 441 by adding from CUL, Ii. 2. 11 chapter and verse numbers, minor corrections and regularisations of spelling, vertical lines to indicate word divisions, most hyphens and all OE rubrics.[161] It is possible, therefore, that in this case the manuscript was used as a printer's copy, although there are no traces of printer's ink on the folios to confirm this.[162] In terms of editorial method, *The Gospels of the Fower Evangelistes* follows *A Testimonie* and the *Archaionomia* in silently conflating manuscript sources which remained completely hidden to the audience. While Parker is mentioned explicitly or implicitly as the collector

---

[155] See https://estc.bl.uk/. [156] Bromwich, 'The First Book', 281.
[157] Lucas, 'A Testimonye', 155–6; Graham, 'The Early Modern Afterlife'. 88–92.
[158] Niles, *The Idea*, 60–2. [159] [Foxe]. *The Gospels*, ¶2r. [160] Skeat, *The Gospel*, xiv.
[161] Ker, *Catalogue*, 376; Graham, 'The Early Modern Afterlife', 95–9. Liuzza, *The Old English Version*, xx. Moreover, they supplied missing text and even missing leaves, including an entire quire (ff. 56–62), possibly using CCCC 140 as a source, as well as a collation of folios and chapter numbers on f. ir.
[162] Graham, 'The Early Modern Afterlife', 99.

and custodian of such ancient monuments, their origins, provenances and peculiarities had no place in the introductions or letters to the reader. The idea of antiquity was not affected by this eclecticism; what to us may seem to be illicit grooming of a manuscript was, to vary on Foxe's words, a reduction of the OE text 'to the Pristine state of olde conformitie'. There is much to discover still in the editorial methods of pioneering figures such as Parker, Joscelyn and Nowell, in terms of what inspired their choices and how they conceptualised OE. What seems clear is that for them editing was tantamount to restoration of antiquity; just as the Church and its doctrines or the state and its laws were to be restored, so were the texts and documents on the basis of which this restoration had to take place.

Around the 1640s a change can be observed in the conventions according to which OE texts were edited. In 1639 Sir Henry Spelman edited various ecclesiastical law texts in the first volume of his *Concilia*, in which he departed from silent emendations, suggesting corrections in the margin, instead.[163] In the following year, John Spelman (1594–1643), Sir Henry's son, published an edition of OE psalter glosses from BL, Stowe 2, which was then in the possession his father. The edition renders the manuscript fairly verbatim, though not without mistakes, printing the Latin psalter text in italics and the OE glosses in an Anglo-Saxon font above the relevant Latin words, which must have been a challenge for the printer, Roger Badger.[164] In the process of editing, John Spelman collated his father's manuscript with three other psalters: CUL, Ff. 1. 23; Cambridge, Trinity College R. 17. 1 (987) and BL, Arundel 60, to which he gave the sigla C., T. and M. Instead of conflating the manuscripts into one version, Spelman inserted collations in the outer margins of the pages which were kept especially wide for this purpose. In the Letter to the Reader, Spelman states explicitly that 'although mistakes are found in all versions, I have ... given you a faithful version of my copy'.[165] The marginal annotations are there to list alternatives or fill in missing text. Thus we read that in Psalm 1.3 *Domini* ('of the Lord') is glossed as *drihtnes* in the Stowe but as *lauorde* in T; *plantatum est* ('is planted') as *plantud is* in Stowe, but *geset is* in T. Occasionally, Spelman makes a critical note, as in Psalm 118.141, where T glosses *Adolescentulus* ('a very young man') as *min ungleæwnes*, to which he adds that this rather translates *mea imprudentia* ('my foolishness').[166] Spelman's edition might be called the first purposely faithful edition of an OE text, in this case glosses, with

---

[163] See, for example, Spelman, *Concilia*, 470 and 574. Brackmann, *Old English Scholarship*, 76.

[164] Ker, *Catalogue*, 336–7.

[165] Spelman, *Psalterium Davidis*, A3v–A4r ('Cúmque omnia exemplaria in pluribus habentur vitiosa, nos ... nostrum tibi exemplar fideliter exhibuimus').

[166] *Ibid.* B1r, Qq3r.

a rudimentary critical apparatus.[167] Although Spelman's edition was not perfect, it was a step forward in editorial scholarship, setting a benchmark that was
observed by Wheelock, who published his 1643 edition of the OE translation of
Bede's *Historia ecclesiastica gentis Anglorum*, from CUL, Kk. 3. 18, which
was his copy text, and added variants, though not consistently, from BL, Cotton
Otho B. xi (badly damaged in the fire of 1731) and CCCC 41, to which he gave
the sigla C and B, respectively.[168] For the *Anglo-Saxon Chronicle*, which he
printed as an appendix to Bede's *Historia ecclesiastica*, Wheelock chose as his
copy text the G version in BL, Cotton Otho B. xi (seven fragments of which
remain) and based his additions on the A-Chronicle from CCCC 173. Here too
his editorial principles are remarkably consistent: all additions and emendations
from A are enclosed in square brackets, even adverbs, prepositions or parts of
words.[169] In the editions of the 1640s, the copy text with marked collations had
become the basis of editorial production; a move away from the eclecticism of
Parker, Nowell and Joscelyn.

The idea of collating texts and manuscripts with the help of sigla also emerges
in the work of Franciscus Junius, whose personal copy of John Spelman's
Psalterium Davidis, now OBL, Junius 33, contains his collations with another
psalter manuscript (OBL, Junius 27), which had been made available to him by
his nephew, Isaac Vossius and to which he consequently gave the siglum
V. Similarly, Junius had become the owner of a copy of Parker's/Foxe's *The
Gospels of the Fower Evangelistes*, now Oxford, Lincoln College Library, N. 1.
7, which he collated with three additional manuscripts containing the OE
Gospels: CUL, Ii. 2. 11, CCCC 140 and OBL, Hatton 38, to which he referred
by the sigla C., B. and H. After underlining the relevant words in the text, Junius
added the corresponding variants mostly in the outer margins; the order in
which the variants are listed is mostly the same: Junius first collated the printed
text with C., then with B. and finally with H. However, rather than indicating all
additions, corrections and emendations, as Wheelock had done, Junius made
additional miscellaneous corrections without reference to a manuscript, expun-
ging single characters, usually i, y, a, t, which he replaced by y, i, æ, d,
respectively, immediately above the expunction. Junius's annotated copy of
The Gospels of the Fower Evangelistes was the basis for the *Quatuor D.N.
J.C. evangeliorum versiones perantiquæ duæ, Goth. scil. et Anglo-Saxonica*, an
edition of the OE Gospels side by side with the Gothic Gospel text from the

---

[167] Bremmer, 'Mine Is Bigger than Yours', 138; Graham, 'Abraham Wheelock', 172, fn. 7.

[168] See Graham, 'Abraham Wheelock', 172, whose detailed discussion addresses for the first time
Wheelock's use of Old English texts in his annotations and ideological purpose of his edition;
Niles, *The Idea*, 113–6.

[169] Lutz, *Die Version G*, lxxiv.

Codex Argenteus, published in 1665. If it had been up to Junius to prepare the edition, he would presumably have offered a sanitised text of OBL, Bodley 441 with collations in the margin.[170] The task of editing the OE Gospels was, however, allocated to the English theologian and polymath Thomas Marshall (1621–84), whose annotations can also be seen in Lincoln College Library, N. 1. 7, adding to and cancelling those by Junius. Marshall incorporated a minority of Junius's collations in the text without referencing and omitted most, but not all, of Junius's silent emendations and corrections.[171] Marshall, whose exceptional philological learning was a hard match for anyone, was only partly successful in rejecting Junius's editorial emendations. The result of the first visible cooperation between two editors of OE texts is a version of the OE Gospels which constitutes, to some extent, a move back to eclecticism.

The long 18th century witnessed the completion of some nine editions of OE texts, eight of which were published between 1698 and 1722. These include editions of the *Anglo-Saxon Chronicle* (1692) by Edmund Gibson (1669–1748); of the *Heptateuch* (the first seven books of the Bible) and other biblical and apocryphal texts (1698) by Edward Thwaites; of Boethius's *De consolatione philosophiae* in OE (1698) by Christopher Rawlinson (1677–1733); of the *Sermo Lupi ad Anglos* (1701) by William Elstob; of Ælfric's *Homily on the Birthday of St Gregory* (1709) by Elizabeth Elstob; of legal texts from the *Textus Roffensis* (1720) by Thomas Hearne; of the Laws of the Anglo-Saxons (1721) by David Wilkins; and of Bede's *Historia ecclesiastica* in OE (1722) by John (1659–1715) and George Smith (1693–1756).[172] One that should be added to this list is the edition of Orosius's *Historiae* in OE by Daines Barrington, which appeared in 1773, but was based on the work of Franciscus Junius, Thomas Marshall and William Elstob. The outburst of activity that produced these editions was boosted by Bishop John Fell and inspired by the work of George Hickes and Humfrey Wanley, both of whom increased an awareness not only of manuscripts containing OE, but also OE texts in early modern transcripts, particularly those by Junius.[173] Each edition should be regarded in the light of its textual history, the scholarly network of its editor(s), its philological methodology and scholarship and the editor's aspirations and motivations.[174]

The challenges which these editions offer to modern scholars are best exemplified by the scholarly appraisal of Elizabeth Elstob's edition of Ælfric's

---

[170] Junius, *Quatuor D.N.J.C. Euangeliorum versiones perantiquæ duæ*; Dekker, 'Francis Junius', 295; see also Lowe, 'William Somner', on the edition of charters.

[171] Dekker, 'Reading the Anglo-Saxon Gospels', 81–7. Niles, *The Idea*, 123–7.

[172] All mentioned by Adams, *Old English Scholarship*, 191–200, and Niles, *The Idea*, 129–34, 165–7.

[173] Lutz, 'The Study', 56–8.

[174] See, for example, Waite, 'John Smith's Edition of Bede's *Historia Ecclesiastica*'.

Homily on the Birthday of St Gregory. The first woman to publish on OE, Elizabeth Elstob's works have attracted a considerable amount of scholarly attention, focusing both on her scholarship and on her drive, courage and pivotally proto-feminist stance. A model of scholarship, Elstob's edition includes an annotated introduction in which she defends Augustine's work as Roman missionary and reconfirms the doctrinal purity of the Anglican church, as well as an annotated anthology of texts pertaining to the Gregorian mission by way of appendix. Equally impressive is her translation of Ælfric's *Homily* into Modern English.[175] At the same time, Elstob's OE text was not based directly on a manuscript, as one might expect, but on a transcript of the homily by William Hopkins, a prebendary of Worcester Cathedral. While Hopkins presumably transcribed from OBL, Hatton 114, Elstob assumed that the transcript was a copy of BL, Cotton Vitellius D. xvii and therefore collated her edition with Hatton 114, thus entering spurious information in her otherwise remarkable *apparatus criticus*. This apparent scholarly shortcoming was explained by Mechthild Gretsch, who shows how important it is to look at Elizabeth Elstob from the perspective of her own time. Not only does Gretsch argue that Elstob's network allowed her access to libraries and manuscripts, but also that Elstob was a child of her times, whose exemplar for her edition of Ælfric's *Homily on the Birthday of St Gregory* was a transcript rather than an original OE manuscript, not because she suffered the difficulties of being female, but because in her (all male) scholarly network this was accepted practice. Christopher Rawlinson's edition of *Boethius* was based on a transcript by Franciscus Junius (OBL, Junius 12); Barrington's edition of *Orosius* used William Elstob's transcript which was itself a copy of Junius's transcript (OBL, Junius 15).[176] Even the *editio princeps* of *Beowulf*, published in Copenhagen by Grímur Jónsson Thorkelin (1752–1829) in 1815, was based on transcripts, one of which was made by an inexpert scribe.

As Thorkelin's edition of *Beowulf* shows, editing OE verse brought its own complications. The question of which poems or verse lines were edited in the 16th, 17th and 18th centuries, and by whom, has been answered by Danielle Cunniff Plumer, whose seminal study maps the progress of editing OE verse and lists all editions in an appendix. Plumer's study makes clear that the editing of OE verse can only be understood against the development of contemporaneous ideas about verse. The first problem that had to be overcome was the difficulty of identifying OE text as verse. In manuscripts, OE verse is invariably written in long lines, mostly indistinguishable from prose, and the earliest editors did not

---

[175] Graham, ed., *Elizabeth Elstob's 'English-Saxon Homily'*, 7.
[176] Gretsch, 'Elizabeth Elstob', 490–3. For the opposite opinion, see Sutherland, 'Editing for a New Century'.

perceive it as verse. Parker's *Ælfredi regis res gestæ* (1574) prints King Alfred's *Metrical Preface* to the OE translation of Gregory's *Regula pastoralis* as prose; there are no indications that its metrical quality was identified. The same can be said for the poems in the *Anglo-Saxon Chronicle*, published by Wheelock, which he designated as passages written in an ancient and rough style that required an effort on the part of the reader. As Plumer and Lucas have argued, Franciscus Junius's 1655 publication of the biblical poetry from the Junius manuscript truly initiated the study of OE verse.[177] Two factors may have contributed to Junius's understanding of OE poetry. The title of Junius's edition, *Cædmonis monachi paraphrasis poetica Genesios ac præcipuarum sacræ paginæ historiarum* ('Cædmon the monk's poetic paraphrase of Genesis and of the main histories in holy scripture'), indicates that he associated the texts in the manuscript with Bede's account of the poet Cædmon and therefore with poetry.[178] This idea may not have been original, since Johannes de Laet, who saw the manuscript before Junius in the early 1640s, not only knew that it contained verse, but also seemed to be aware of the interpolation now known as *Genesis B*.[179] The manuscript's former owner, James Ussher, will therefore have known it, but it was Junius who formalised its connection with Cædmon. The other factor is Junius's comprehension of the system of pointing which separated the metrical half lines in the Junius manuscript – a system which he managed to apply fruitfully to his transcript of *Judith* in OBL, Junius 105, where he used a combination of punctuation and extended spaces to demarcate the verse.[180] Although Junius printed the biblical poems in long lines, as in the manuscript, and the edition offered no other help to the reader whatsoever, the visibility of the half lines through the system of metrical pointing allowed readers to think about OE verse for the first time. Junius copied much more OE verse, including the metres of Boethius from BL, Cotton Otho A. vi, which were transcribed in OBL, Junius 12. Christopher Rawlinson printed the OE *Boethius*, including the metres, from Junius 12, and was the first to print metrical half lines in a vertical arrangement, so not side by side, separated by a caesura, as in modern editions. In his preface, Rawlinson informed his readers of King Alfred's potential authorship and stated that he separated the verse lines in order to display them; the verse, however, is in Rawlinson's opinion not as good as Cædmon's. Rawlinson's manner of printing OE verse was adopted by

---

[177] Plumer, 'The Construction of Structure', 243–5; Niles, *The Idea*, 65–70.

[178] See Frantzen, *Desire*, 155, who states that the idea of Cædmon's authorship of all biblical poetry in OE goes back to John Bale. Niles, *The Idea*, 116–20.

[179] Bremmer, 'Mine Is Bigger than Yours', 152.

[180] Plumer, 'The Construction of Structure', 255–9; Lucas, 'Franciscus Junius and the Versification of *Judith*', 372–5; Dekker, *Anglo-Saxon, Norse and Celtic*, 21–5.

George Hickes in his *Thesaurus*, pp. 177–208, and by Wanley in his *Catalogue*, although both also printed verse in long lines. With the exception of *The Battle of Maldon*, printed by Thomas Hearne in his 1726 edition of the *Chronicle* of John of Glastonbury (pp. 570–7), Hickes's *Thesaurus* was the last publication offering unpublished OE verse, including lines 1–20, 53–74 of *Beowulf* and the (now lost) *Finnsburh Fragment*, before Thorkelin's *Beowulf*.[181]

The comparatively large number of editions of OE texts that came out during the early modern period raises the inevitable question of readership. Annotations, owner's names, entries in library sales catalogues and lists of subscribers may provide some insight into buyers and owners, but the number of buyers who could actually read the OE text must have been small. More work needs to be done on print-runs, sales, citations and usage. Nonetheless, editing was considered important and was promoted by pivotal sponsors of OE studies such as Matthew Parker, Sir Henry Spelman and John Fell. If we survey published editions and aborted plans, two observations present themselves: first, the edited OE texts were nearly all accessible in Latin as well. Secondly, most early modern editions of OE texts fitted the religious or historical motives that drove the study of OE during this period: the wish to connect the English Church and state and law to an Anglo-Saxon past.

5 Studying Old English

In his 2017 discussion of grammars of Arabic, the literary historian Alastair Hamilton states that 'one of the more mystifying aspects of the grammars of ancient and Oriental languages produced in the West during the Renaissance is how students were expected to proceed'. Hamilton's question is as relevant for OE as it is for the early modern study of Arabic, since, like Arabic, OE was first studied for ideological reasons.[182] In fact, it is even more mystifying how early modern students managed to get a grip on OE, given that there were no grammars of instruction at all. The wide availability of primers, introductions and text books of OE in this day and age has blurred our view of the difficulties early modern scholars must have faced. Early modern descriptions of the activities involved in the study of OE are rare: most famous and much cited is William L'Isle's practical advice or pseudo-curriculum in the introduction to his *Saxon Treatise Concerning the Old and New Testament* from 1623. L'Isle's 'earnest desire to know what learning lay hid in this old English tongue', triggered 'this vneasie way' of first acquainting himself with 'the Dutch both high and low' (in modern terms: High German and Low German or Dutch), then

---

[181] Plumer, 'The Construction of Structure', 262–6, 272.
[182] Hamilton. 'The Qu'ran as Chrestomathy', 213–15.

to read 'old English' poetry and prose, by which L'Isle meant Middle English, and then, more than once, from beginning to end, Gavin Douglas's Older Scots 762-page translation of Virgil's *Æneid* (the *Eneados*, London, 1553). Subsequently, L'Isle turned to the Ten Commandments in OE, followed by Parker's *Testimonie of Antiquitie* and Foxe's 1571 edition of the OE Gospels. Only then did he find himself 'able (as it were to swimme without bladders) to vnderstand the vntranslated fragments of the tongue'.[183] Approaching a new language through comparing texts with translations in a familiar language was a tried method used not only for studying Greek or Arabic, but also for OE. It is not surprising, therefore, that texts easily accessible in Latin, such as the Paternoster, Gospels, psalter and Bede's OE *Historia Ecclesiastica*, functioned as Rosetta Stones for the earliest students of OE. Matthew Parker noted in his manuscript of the bilingual Rule of St Benedict (CCCC 178, part II) that 'in this book, the Saxon language can be learned quite easily'.[184]

Rather than a method for the study of OE, L'Isle's observations should perhaps be regarded as an implicit comment on the want of a grammar of OE, which, at the time, was keenly felt. In part, this lack was compensated for by the scholars' superb knowledge of Latin grammar. The principles of Latin grammar were regarded as a universal tool and template for describing and learning other languages, and OE was no exception. However, as we will see in George Hickes's *Institutiones grammaticæ Anglo-Saxonicæ, et Moesogothicæ*, the first printed grammar of OE which came out in 1689, this method had its limitations, leading to such idiosyncratic notions as the construction of declensions for the vocative and ablative cases in OE nouns and a separate section for the construction of the passive verb conjugations.[185] Moreover, the dominance of Latin, Greek and classical grammatical categories coloured the study of OE throughout the early modern period, not only in the field of grammar, but also that of poetics and the first explorations into textual criticism. The incorporation of OE into comparative Germanic philology, from the middle of the 17th century onwards, produced some cracks in this classical vase, but it did not break it. Joseph Bosworth's *Elements of Anglo-Saxon Grammar* from 1823 no longer lists vocatives and ablatives for the nominal declensions, but is still a product of the 18th century when it comes to describing the adjectives.[186] With so much material about the actual study of OE still available only in manuscript, the question of how students of OE proceeded during the early modern period has, so far, generated only incomplete answers.

---

[183] L'Isle, *A Saxon Treatise*, c4v–d1r. Niles, *The Idea*, 110–13.

[184] Graham, 'The Beginnings', 37; Berkhout, 'Laurence Nowell and the Old English Bede'.

[185] Hickes, *Institutiones*, 11–12 (on the nominal declensions), 59–60 (on the passive verb).

[186] Bosworth, *The Elements*, 88–102, lists only the paradigm for the strong declension.

With no early modern grammars of OE to go by, the earliest generations of scholars and students of OE relied on a grammar of Latin written shortly before 1000 AD by the monk, scholar and pedagogue Ælfric of Eynsham. Remarkably for that time, Ælfric composed his *Grammar* in OE, consistently translating the many examples of Latin words, declensions and constructions, as well as some of the rules he took from his source.[187] By reading the grammar backwards, as it were, going from the Latin to the OE, it was possible to extract information about the translation of an OE word as well as the grammatical functions expressed by its inflections. According to R. E. Buckalew, Robert Talbot, whose annotations to Ælfric's *Grammar* can be observed in CUL, Hh. 1. 10, 'could make the *Grammatica* his basic OE textbook, as a number of others did after him', thereby 'reversing the original purpose of the *Grammar* from teaching Latin to learning OE'.[188] However, the question of whether or not Ælfric's *Grammar* is suitable for learning OE has been a matter of debate. In his Latin preface, Ælfric seems to suggest that he intended his *Grammar* to support his novices' Latin as well as English, but, as Helmut Gneuss has made clear, Ælfric's *Grammar* does not describe OE, but gives pupils the grammatical tools, in the form of proper terminology, to describe their language.[189] For anyone learning OE during the early modern period, the *Grammar's* limited descriptive value must have been problematic. Thus, we learn that OE *cempa* 'fighter' equals Latin *miles, militis*; *gesið* 'companion' stands for *comes, comitis*; *wealhstod* 'interpreter' for *interpres, interpretis*, but Ælfric did not explain – nor did he need to – that the genitive singulars in OE were *cempan, gesiþes* and *wealhstodes*. In the case of pronouns, Ælfric's *Grammar* is more helpful: see for example the translations of Latin *idem* 'the same', *se ilca; eiusdem, þæs ylcan; eidem, þæm ylcan; eundem, þone ylcan; ab eodem, fram þam ylcan ...,* which provides almost the entire declension of determiners, as well as the declensions of weak adjectives.[190] However, for all of its useful information, converting Ælfric's *Grammar* into anything like a usable primer of OE still required substantial work on the part of the user; moreover, no printed edition of it was published until 1659.

Despite these obvious problems with its structure and pedagogical value, Ælfric's *Grammar* was very much on the horizon of early modern scholars. It was already noticed by John Leland, who reported a manuscript of it in his *Collectanea*, perhaps BL, Cotton Faustina A. x. The same holds for Leland's contemporary, Robert Talbot, who inserted underlinings and marginalia in

---

[187] The *Exerptiones de Prisciano*, a 10th-century abbreviation of *Institutiones grammaticæ* by the 5th-century grammarian Priscian.

[188] Buckalew, 'Nowell, Lambarde and Leland', 19.

[189] Menzer, 'Ælfric's English Grammar', 109, who cites Gneuss, 'The Study of Language', 14.

[190] Zupitza, *Ælfrics Grammatik*, 51, 106–7.

CUL, Hh. 1. 10.[191] The earliest firm indication that Ælfric's *Grammar* was being used as a tool for the study of OE is presumably Laurence Nowell's partly abridged transcript of it (now London, Westminster Abbey, MS 30), made before 1565, the year in which he gave it to William Lambarde.[192] Its exemplar has never been conclusively identified, partly because of Nowell's editorial changes. As Ker's *Catalogue* indicates, manuscripts of Ælfric's *Grammar* were owned or used by many prominent scholars of OE. Matthew Parker owned CUL, Hh. 1. 10 (his hand appears on fol. 41 v), CCCC 449 and Cambridge, Trinity College R. 9, 17, which he left to his son John.[193] Helmut Gneuss suggests that a deluxe 16th-century transcript on parchment (now Cambridge, Trinity College R. 9. 8 [812]) was made for Matthew Parker (presumably from BL, Royal 15. B. XII).[194] John Joscelyn annotated CUL, Hh. 1. 10 and probably used Durham, Cathedral Library, B. iii. 32 for his lexicographical notes in London, Lambeth Palace 692.[195] Abraham Wheelock claimed to have retrieved CUL, Hh. 1. 10, which contains annotations in his hand, after it had been stolen from Cambridge University Library and also used BL, Cotton Faustina A. x.[196] Sir Henry Spelman was acquainted with two manuscripts of the *Grammar*: BL, Cotton Julius A. ii and Faustina A. x.[197] Sir Simonds D'Ewes owned BL, Harley 107, which was transcribed for him into what is now BL, Harley 589, art 47; Harley 107 was also transcribed by Gerard Langbaine (1608/9–58) into what is now OBL, e Musaeo 161.[198] D'Ewes also transcribed CUL, Hh. 1. 10 and collated it with Cambridge, Trinity College R. 9. 17; this is now BL, Harley 8; Franciscus Junius (or Gerard Langbaine) then collated D'Ewes's transcript with BL, Royal 15 B. XXII.[199] The latter manuscript was William Somner's copy text for his edition added to his *Dictionarium Saxonico-Latino-Anglicum*. Franciscus Junius's personal copy of Somner's *Dictionarium* (OBL, Junius 7) includes collations of Somner's edition with CUL, Hh. 1. 10 and BL, Harley 107. The list suggests that most of the manuscripts of Ælfric's *Grammar* known or used in early modern England were regularly consulted by scholars of OE.[200] It would appear, therefore, that the *Grammar*'s shortcomings were not insurmountable to the relatively small group of scholars that was interested in OE. Moreover,

---

[191] Buckalew, 'Nowell, Lambarde and Leland', 20.

[192] Gneuss in Zupitza, *Ælfrics Grammatik*, ix.

[193] Graham, 'Matthew Parker's Manuscripts', 331.

[194] Gneuss in Zupitza, *Ælfrics Grammatik*, viii.

[195] Ker, *Catalogue*, 22; Graham, 'John Joscelyn', 139, fn. 4.

[196] Ker, *Catalogue*, 22; Hetherington, *The Beginnings*, 85.   [197] Lutz, 'Study', 33.

[198] Gneuss in Zupitza, *Ælfrics Grammatik*, viii–ix.

[199] Bennett, *The Beginnings*, 340. Gneuss in Zupitza, *Ælfrics Grammatik*, viii.

[200] The list here is not meant to be exhaustive.

Somner's decision to append an edition of the *Grammar* to his *Dictionarium* proliferated the text after 1659.

The role of Ælfric's *Grammar* as a source of information also appears in new grammars which were produced from the late 16th century onwards. The first of those was presumably John Joscelyn's grammar; it is now lost, but we know that it existed from references to it. Together with Joscelyn's dictionary volumes, the *Grammar* ended up in Sir Robert Cotton's Library, from which it was lent first to William Camden in 1612 and subsequently to Sir Henry Spelman in and around 1615.[201] Joscelyn's grammar had definitely disappeared in 1689, when George Hickes reported in the preface to his *Institutiones grammaticæ* that it was missing. In preparation of his grammar, Joscelyn studied Ælfric's *Grammar* in CUL Hh. 1. 10: his annotations to that manuscript include repetitions in the margins of grammatical pointers from Ælfric's text, for example, *nomina diriuativa, nomina propria, nomina appellatiua* (fol. 4 v) ('derivative nouns, proper names, proper nouns'), which allowed him to retrieve the relevant data for his own use (see Figure 8). An index compiled by John Parker (now OBL, Bodley 33), who may have wished to publish it, provides an idea of its scope, contents and size: 220 pages (or folia).[202] From a small sample printed by Hetherington, it appears that some of the OE forms occur in Ælfric's *Grammar*, for example '*Wæg. Viam.*'; '*Wæge. Lanx. cis.*'; '*Wæpman. M. Mas.*'; '*Wære. Fuiße*', while other entries can be linked to OE texts with Latin glosses: '*Wæles clænes. Gurgitis puri.*' and '*Wælhreowne worulde. Cruentum Saeculum Accus.*' occur in OE glossed hymns, while the entry '*Wæg. ealne. Viam omnem.*' can be traced to a glossed prayer from BL, Arundel 155.[203] However, most of these forms also occur in Joscelyn's *Dictionarium*,[204] which suggests that for Joscelyn grammar and lexicography went hand-in-hand. This may explain Joscelyn's custom of listing different morphological forms of the same semantic lemma in his dictionary: '*wealdan*' not only means '*dominari*' but is an infinitive; '*wealdað dominantur*' is the form of the indicative plural.[205] John Parker's index also contains grammar rules generated from this information: in a section titled *Secvndvs index alphabeticus de regulis*, Parker observed, for example, that 'in the nominal declension -a is always the ending of the genitive plural'.[206] It is unclear, however, whether these extrapolations were Parker's or Joscelyn's; at the same time, it shows that their grammatical thinking incorporated attempts at analysing the data and drawing up rules for their own benefit and that of others.

---

[201] Lucas, 'The Earliest Modern Anglo-Saxon Grammar', 381–2.

[202] Graham, 'John Joscelyn', 94–5.

[203] Hetherington, *The Beginnings*, 186–8; OBL, Bodley 33, f. 109r; *DOEC*, svv.

[204] See BL, Cotton Titus A. xv, ff. 246r–274.   [205] BL, Cotton Titus A. xv, f. 254v.

[206] OBL, Bodley 33, f. 117r.

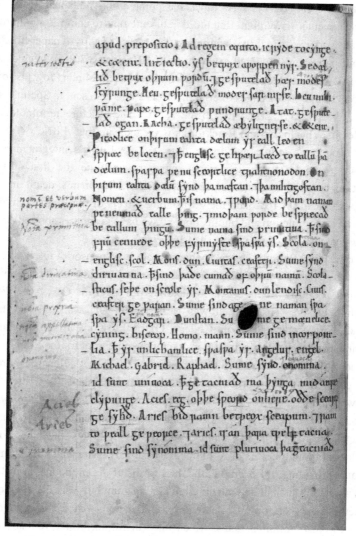

Figure 8 Cambridge, University Library, Hh 1. 10, f. 4v

Renewed attempts to produce OE grammars in the second and third quarters of the 17th century still focused largely on the use of Ælfric's *Grammar*. This time, the inspiration came from Sir Henry Spelman, whose plans for the Cambridge lectureship founded in 1639 included the compilation of an OE grammar, besides a dictionary.[207] Spelman left the task to Abraham Wheelock, the first incumbent of his lectureship, whose 1643 edition of the OE Bede contains notes on grammar

---

[207] Lutz, 'The Study', 35.

in the *Ad lectorem* (B2 v).[208] As Lucas has pointed out, Wheelock engaged his pupil and amanuensis William Retchford in his attempts to compile a grammar of OE. Their work exists in three documents: (1) a series of slips of paper filled with notes and paradigms mounted at the back of BL, Harley 761 (Wheelock's OE lexicon), (2) a nine-page fair copy of a grammar sent to Spelman (now part of BL, Add. 35333) and (3) ten pages of critical observations also sent to Spelman (now BL, Add. 34600, 211r, 212r, 213r, 215r–218r).[209] The structure, terminology and examples in Wheelock's and Retchford's work indicate that Ælfric's *Grammar* was an important source and inspiration. Yet, as Lucas's integrated edition demonstrates, these three documents together constitute the first surviving attempt to compile a grammar of OE.[210] Sadly, Spelman's death in 1641, Wheelock's death in 1653 and the devastating effects of the English Civil War prevented its completion and publication; all we have is another aborted attempt, and one that was even less visible than Joscelyn's.

After the Civil War, Sir Henry Spelman's role as a sponsor of OE studies was assumed by Bishop John Fell of Oxford, who founded the Oxford University Press and acquired Junius's Anglo-Saxon types to print OE. According to William Nicolson, 'Bishop Fell was earnest with Dr. Marshall [= Thomas Marshall, late Rector of Lincoln College, Oxford] to draw up a grammar; and he [Marshall] devolved the work upon one much more unfit for the Employment, who had made some collections to that purpose'.[211] These 'collections' are four leaves of notes on OE morphology, now in OBL, Marshall 78, written by an unknown scribe. Divided into sections titled '*verba*', '*genera*', '*pronomina*', '*nomina*' and '*particula*', the notes display mostly paradigms derived partly or completely from Ælfric's *Grammar*, which was definitely the basis for this compilation, though not its only source. Occasionally, Marshall's hand inserted additions, providing, for example, the dual forms of the pronouns. Four further leaves in OBL, Marshall 78 with notes on Gothic grammar were clearly meant to complement the work on OE. There are no indications that anything more was done with these grammar notes, which may, therefore, be the remnant of yet another aborted OE grammar project. However, the notes in OBL, Marshall 78 are the first attempt at an OE grammar on a comparative basis.

The grammar notes in OBL, Marshall 78 suggest that, by 1665, times had changed for the study of OE grammar. These changes had come not from England but from the Continent, where in the late 16th century humanist interest in language comparison merged with an increasing awareness of 'Germanic' as an identity concept. In the Low Countries, particularly, connecting the

---

[208] This information was reprinted in Somner, *Dictionarium*, b2rv.

[209] Lucas, 'The Earliest Modern Anglo-Saxon Grammar', 383–7.   [210] *Ibid.* 386–417.

[211] Nicolson, *The English Historical Library*, 101.

vernacular with Gothic and other Germanic languages fostered historical and political self-awareness. Right from the start, OE was part of this developing new world view. The discovery of the *Codex Argenteus* in the early 1550s,[212] a budding antiquarian interest in runes and the earliest editions of Old High German and OE texts occasioned the publication in 1599 of *De literis & lingua Getarum sive Gothorum* by Bonaventura Vulcanius, in which OE was represented by a reprint of King Alfred's preface to Gregory's *Pastoral Care*, as printed by Parker in his *Alfredi regis res gestæ*. Vulcanius's *De literis* was the first book that printed an OE text, albeit not with Anglo-Saxon letters, for the purpose of comparing it with other (Germanic) languages, including Gothic. The seeds planted by Vulcanius came to fruition in the works of Franciscus Junius, whose copy of *De literis* features among his books and manuscripts in the Bodleian Library.[213] Junius's study of OE grammar can be observed in his etymological glossaries, in which he compared OE with Gothic, Old High German, Old Low Franconian, 'Runic' (an umbrella term for the Oldest Scandinavian dialects), Old Frisian, as well as with Welsh, Modern English and Dutch and, very prominently, with Greek.[214] In his *Observationes in Willerami* from 1655, Junius argued that OE should be seen as one of three Germanic branches (the other two being Gothic and Old High German) and that English, Scots, Dutch and Frisian derived from it.[215] Linguistically, Junius' methodology of language comparison included the idea of *detruncatio* ('exposing the stem by cutting it free'): the formal relation between OE and its relatives could be understood if one considered the stem syllables of words. His list of 73 'OE monosyllables as if broken off of the beginning of Greek words' constitutes the first genuine attempt at OE etymology. For example, Junius considered OE '*æðm*, Vapor' to be related to Greek ἀτμὸς, 'Flatus, halitus, vapor', and OE '*bræs, Æs.* English *brasse.* Welsh *pres.*' to be cut from Greek πράσιος, a word linked by Junius to πράσινος 'green', due to the green colour of the copper ore.[216] Although based on a phonic resemblance of word stems, Junius's concept of etymology was far removed from modern linguistic methodology and from contemporary rationalist ideas. Instead, it included word fields and semantics as well as what we now know as morphology. One could argue that for Junius etymology comprised the study of most observable language features: from letters and their corresponding sounds to the meaning of words and phrases. Old English grammar was, therefore, part of his etymological thinking,

---

[212] See p. 31.

[213] OBL, Junius 98. See Dekker, *The Origins*, 205–18 and *passim* on Van Vliet.

[214] Dekker, *Anglo-Saxon, Norse and Celtic*, 10–20.   [215] Dekker, *The Origins*, 258.

[216] Junius, *Observationes*, 233–58, at 234, 235. 'Monosyllaba Anglo-Saxonica e Græcarum vocum principio veluti abrupta'. Dekker, *Anglo-Saxon, Norse and Celtic*, 16.

as various etymological glossaries indicate. For example, in the entry on 'I, Ego', in the *Etymologicum Anglicanum*, Junius lists the reflexes in Gothic, OE, Alemannic, French, Italian, Spanish, Norse, Danish, Dutch and Greek, before citing part of Ælfric's *Grammar* to inform us that the pronoun inflections in OE reveal the variation of number and case.[217] Following the lead, Edward Lye, the editor of the *Etymologicum Anglicanum*, added the forms of other pronouns. Similarly, in Junius's *Gothicum Glossarium*, we are taught that the Gothic dual pronoun *IGGUIS* is *inc* in OE and that the OE forms *cuð*, *muð* and *toð* all correspond to forms with an *n* in Gothic and other West Germanic languages (cf. Dutch *kond*, *mond*, *tand*) – an early description of Ingvaeonic lengthening.[218] Primarily, Junius's etymologies were meant to demonstrate that ancient wisdom or *antiquitas* could be found by means of a philological comparison of words – an aim that lay at the basis of all his etymological glossaries.[219] However, in the process of reaching this philosophical aim, he produced observations about OE grammar which suggest that, like others before him, he had internalised Ælfric's *Grammar*.

The result of Junius's influence on the study of OE grammar is seen not only in the work of his closest collaborators, such as Thomas Marshall, but particularly in the publications of George Hickes. In 1689, George Hickes, who had been Marshall's confidant and student at Lincoln College,[220] published his *Institutiones Grammaticæ Anglo-Saxonicæ et Moeso-Gothicæ*. The title of Hickes's book covers only the first part: a grammar of OE and Gothic. This was followed, however, by the Icelandic grammar by Runólfur Jónsson (1620–54), a small dictionary of Icelandic based on words from the grammar, the *Catalogus veterum librorum septentrionalium*, Edward Bernard's *Etymologicon Britannicum* and a double page of alphabets. As Hughes has demonstrated, Hickes's work on OE grammar is descriptive rather than elementary or pedagogical and depends on the Latin grammarians Donatus and Priscian for its organisation, terminology and paradigmatic structure.[221] After explaining the alphabets, Hickes moved through the various word classes, beginning with the article, and going from there to nouns and adjectives, pronouns, verbs and participles, adverbs, conjunctions, prepositions and interjections. In each section he first provided the OE forms, followed by notes on orthographical variants and exceptions, and then continued with an overview of the same forms in Gothic, which is invariably more concise. The Latin template and descriptive nature of the grammar implied that while Hickes produced an unprecedented quantity of

---

[217] Junius, *Etymologicum Anglicanum*, ed. Lye, kkk2v.

[218] Junius, *Gothicum glossarium*, 62, 207.

[219] Romburgh, ''How to Make the Past Age Present', 166–8.   [220] Harris, *A Chorus*, 4–8.

[221] Hughes, 'The Anglo-Saxon Grammars', 121–2. Niles, *The Idea*, 123–5.

information, he probably never investigated the OE language for its own principles and peculiarities beyond the framework of Latin. Therefore, the adjectives with their different declensions depending on definite or indefinite usage were not properly understood by him, and the variety of verb conjugations remains unexplained: a separate chapter on *beon* 'to be' is followed by two chapters on the active and passive verb forms, respectively, and a short chapter on 'impersonal verbs'. In the final chapter on verbs (XI), Hickes provides an unstructured list of what he considered to be irregular verbs, conceding that 'there are many verbs in the ancestral language that deviate from the norm of the given paradigm'.[222] A final, additional chapter (XVIII) lists Icelandic grammatical paradigms with the goal of comparing them with OE and Gothic. This chapter is the first etymological study of function words and bound morphemes and constitutes Hickes's personal contribution to the idea of a Germanic language family. Its focus on language comparison connects this chapter with his *Præfatio ad lectorem*, which describes the Germanic language family and reads like a dedication to Fell, Marshall and Junius who had in different ways been Hickes's inspiration. As the first published grammatical study of OE, Hickes's *Institutiones* are a vital step in the development of OE philology. It was, however, not a book of instruction. Its grammar remains difficult to access, and despite being called *institutiones*, a term with clear educational connotations, it contains no texts to help a reader build up a reading knowledge of OE. Nonetheless, as Bennett claims, 'there is much evidence of its use'.[223]

Hickes's *Institutiones* were followed in 1703–5 by his *Linguarum Veterum septentrionalium thesaurus grammatico-criticus et archæologicus*. Even without Wanley's *Catalogue* of manuscripts, which was sometimes bound in a separate volume, the contents of Hickes's *Thesaurus* were awe-inspiring in its time, as well as today. Born out of Hickes's wish to publish a second edition of the *Institutiones*, the *Thesaurus* is, in the first place 'a chorus of grammars': OE – Gothic – Old High German (or *Franco-Theotisca* as Hickes termed it) – and Icelandic.[224] Secondly, it is a history and encyclopaedia of the OE language, literature and culture, in a comparative, Germanic framework and, thirdly, the first book that genuinely theorises *in extenso* about OE in a variety of aspects. The first part of the *Thesaurus* is titled *Institutiones grammaticæ Anglo-Saxonicæ, & Mœso-Gothicæ* (pp. 1–235), just like the 1689 grammar. It

---

[222] Hickes, *Institutiones*, 66: 'multa sunt verba in linguâ Majorum quæ à normâ dati paradigmatis deflectunt'.

[223] Bennett, *The History*, 56.

[224] As Hickes phrased it in his letter to Arthur Charlett from 7 July 1696. Harris, *A Chorus*, 63. On pp. 39–107 Harris provides a vivid and detailed account of the conception, preparation and execution of the *Thesaurus*. Niles, *The Idea*, 148–56.

includes all eighteen chapters from the earlier version, with mostly the same paradigms but with more explanatory text. However, in the *Thesaurus*, Hickes more than doubled the *Institutiones* by adding six more chapters, on OE dialectology and poetics. Described in some detail by Harris, Hickes's final chapters present the first scholarly, theoretical discussions of these topics.[225] The idea of dialects based on orthographical, morphological and lexical differences between OE texts had been toyed with by Junius and had been the topic of a chapter in William Nicolson's *English Historical Library*.[226] Inspired by Nicolson's ideas, Hickes distinguished between 'Britanno-Saxon' (the earliest OE language, dating from the 6th, 7th and 8th centuries, of which there were hardly any written records) and variants which had come about through the influence of historical and demographic events. The Danish incursions gave rise to 'Dano-Saxon' in the north and east, while a 'pure Saxon' endured in the south and west of England in the works of King Alfred, Ælfric and Wulfstan. As a result of the influence of the Danes and the Norman Conquest, 'pure Saxon' degenerated into 'Semi-Saxon', visible, for example in the 12th-century entries in the *Peterborough Chronicle*.[227] The final phase in his dialectology of OE was termed 'Normanno-Saxon', which he illustrated with the help of citations from, for example, the *Ormulum*, a text which we nowadays classify as early Middle English. Hickes's scope of OE, then, is chronologically more extended than that of today and included the phase of what he regarded as OE in its later, corrupted stage. Hickes, like others, believed in a golden age of OE and a decline after the Norman Conquest.

A similar scope and development can be seen in Hickes's chapters on OE verse, which discuss the influence of the Norse tradition (ch. 21), the core system of OE verse (ch. 23) and the developments in 'Semi-Saxon' or corrupted verse, which would eventually lead to the *poesis nostra Anglicana*, or Middle English poetry (ch. 24). These additional chapters differ from the previous ones in that they depart from the comparative framework of the grammar and focus predominantly on English. Moreover, whereas the earlier part of the grammar features relatively few texts, the final six offer an exciting anthology of texts and fragments, both in prose and verse, many of which had never been printed before, including items now lost such as the OE *Rune Poem* and the *Finnsburh Fragment*.[228] Hickes's attempt at writing an OE *poetica* in chapter twenty-three is one of the most remarkable chapters in the history of OE studies. As Plumer and Lucas have indicated, an understanding of OE verse began in earnest with Franciscus Junius, whose edition of biblical poems and transcript of *Judith*

---

[225] Harris, *A Chorus*, 72–9.   [226] Nicolson, *The English Historical Library*, 102.

[227] Cain, 'George Hickes', provides a detailed discussion of Hickes's dialectology of OE.

[228] Hickes, *Thesaurus*, 135–6, 192; Niles, *The Idea*, 176–82.

betrayed an insight into OE metre which earlier scholars, including Wheelock and Somner, did not have.[229] However, although Junius was able to identify verse and correctly added punctuation separating verse units which were undistinguished in the manuscripts, he did not theorise. Hickes's approach to OE verse was very different. Essentially, it resembled his approach to grammar: in either case classical (Greek and Latin) patterns formed the basis of his thinking. Both Shannon McCabe's doctoral work, with a full translation of chapter twenty-three of the *Thesaurus*, and Seth Lerer's analysis of Hickes's metrics against the Greek poetry of Pindar have demonstrated that in Hickes's view OE verse, like OE grammar, had to be measurable by classical standards.[230] The key to understanding OE verse patterns lay, according to Hickes, in the recognition of rhythm, feet and tempos, which had to be viewed together with poetic language: both vocabulary and syntax. Alliteration and assonance were regarded as ornamental.

Despite Hickes's failure to understand OE verse, the *Thesaurus* is a monumental publication in the history of OE scholarship. It crowns a century of fruitful exchange between English and continental scholars culminating in a storehouse of learing about the ancient Northern (read Germanic) languages. Of those, Old Norse gained particular prominence, as we can see in Hickes's dedication to Prince George of Denmark which ends with a citation from the *Völuspá*. Not only was Old Norse genetically related to OE, but its influence – as Hickes illustrated – also extended to language contact, resulting in the Dano-Saxon dialect, and to literary influence: Hickes felt, for example, that the metre of *The Finnsburh Fragment* resembled that of the 13th-century *Hervarar saga ok Heiðreks*.[231] Similarly, Wanley's *Catalogue* prints a list of *manuscripta Scandica* (containing Old Norse historical texts) from the Royal Library in Stockholm sent to Hickes by the Swedish antiquarian Johann Peringskjöld (1654–1720), followed by excerpts from correspondence about Old Norse books and texts between Hickes and the Swedish historian Jonas Nicolaus Salanus (1664–1706).[232] The attention to Old Norse texts and manuscripts in the *Thesaurus* indicates how important the study of Old Norse had become in England, where, in 1670, Robert Sheringham's *De Anglorum gentis origine disceptatio*, made use of Norse sources to describe the migration history of the Goths, as ancestors of the Angles, Saxons and Jutes.[233] The other way round, Hickes's *Thesaurus* was mentioned prominently in Johannes Ihre's *Glossarium Suiogothicum* (1769), an etymological dictionary of Swedish in

[229] See p. 45. [230] McCabe, 'Anglo-Saxon Poetics'; Lerer, 'The Anglo-Saxon Pindar'.

[231] Hickes, *Thesaurus*, ††††r, 193. Graham, 'Old English and Old Norse Studies', 18.

[232] Wanley, *Catalogus*, 310–21; Harris, *A Chorus*, 53–63.

[233] See Graham, 'Old English and Old Norse Studies', for the history and influence of Old Norse studies in England from the middle of the 17th century.

which OE cognates abound. Notwithstanding its panoramic view of northern studies, OE remains very much at the centre of the *Thesaurus*, which graced the bookshelves of most, if not all academic libraries and would be the determining factor of OE studies in the 18th century.[234]

Hickes's curriculum for the study of OE – the second after L'Isle's – in the preface to his grammar of Old English and Gothic indicates that he also saw a role for the *Thesaurus* as a manual of instruction. For most students, however, the *Thesaurus* was well out of reach, owing to its price and probably its size. Two elementary grammars of OE intended for instruction appeared within a decade after Hickes's *Thesaurus*. The first, a forty-eight-page Latin outline of the *Grammatica Anglo-Saxonica & Moeso-Gothica* in Hickes's *Thesaurus*, titled *Grammatica Saxonica*, was published in 1711 by Edward Thwaites, whose foundational role as a teacher and influencer of OE studies in the early 18th century stands out. As praeceptor in Anglo-Saxon at Queen's College, Oxford, Thwaites taught OE in extracurricular classes where the students were made to work hard, as Thwaites was convinced that 'the morals and industry of young scholars are kept up by the vigilance of the tutor'.[235] Thwaites's famous outcry in 1699, that for fifteen young students in his class he had only one copy of Somner's dictionary, indicated the need for affordable and appropriate descriptions of OE, both lexicographical and grammatical. It was Thwaites, therefore, who enabled Thomas Benson to publish his *Vocabularium* in 1701,[236] while ten years later he published the first student grammar of OE. The information in Thwaites's *Grammatica Saxonica* is purely Hickesian, but omits the comparative component. The same applies to Elizabeth Elstob's *The Rudiments of Grammar for the English-Saxon Tongue*, published in 1715, the first grammar of OE written in English, for which Elstob, who was an outstanding calligrapher, designed the Old English font.[237] In the words of Shaun Hughes, Elstob's OE grammar is not only the first one published in English, 'but also the first grammar to be mindful of the reader'.[238] Dedicated to Caroline of Ansbach, Princess of Wales, Elstob's grammar is, as Gretsch and Hughes have argued, an ambitious amalgamation of the grammars by Hickes and Thwaites with Ælfric's *Grammar*, from which Elstob took renewed inspiration.[239] While Elstob's grammar does not offer innovation in terms of paradigms and substance, she stimulated readers

---

[234] The list of subscribers at the end of Wanley's *Catalogus* shows the destinations of copies. The universities of Oxford and Cambridge feature prominently.

[235] Bennett, *The History*, 69; Frazier Wood, *Anglo-Saxonism*, 20–2.

[236] Lowe, 'Somner, *Gavelkind* and Lexicography', 284. See p. 27.

[237] Hollis, 'On the Margins', 158.   [238] Hughes, 'The Anglo-Saxon Grammars', 120.

[239] *Ibid.* 122–3; Gretsch, 'Elizabeth Elstob', 513–14; Sutherland, 'Elizabeth Elstob', 67; Niles, *The Idea*, 160–2.

through the presentation of her work, its use of Modern English instead of Latin, schematic layout, brevity of style and didactic approach. In addition to being a formidable scholar and a judicious author who wrote lengthy, argumentative prefaces, Elstob was also a natural teacher whose introductions to essential topics in OE are timeless. Adapting the first lines of Hickes's second chapter, Elstob introduced the articles in OE in her engaging, didactic style: 'As the Greeks and other nations have had their articles placed before their nouns, so the *Saxon* Tongue hath used hers, both with Skill and Beauty. These are naturally to be consider'd according to their Cases or Endings, before we treat the nouns' (see Figure 9).[240] On page iii of her thirty-five-page preface Elstob outlined her pedagogical approach, explaining that her intended audience consisted of those whose education, 'hath not allow'd them an Acquaintance with the Grammars of other Languages', a reference to the female readership that she had in mind.[241] No other grammar of OE had been written from a similar starting point, explicit instruction, rather than description, and no other grammar of OE had been linked so openly to contemporary political, cultural and literary ideas.

While the grammars of Thwaites and Elstob ensured access to OE grammar both for Latinate university students and for those who came to OE from a monolingual English background, they also ossified the study of OE. Two outlines of OE grammar prefaced to Edward Lye's edition of Junius's *Etymologicum Anglicanum* (1743) and to Lye and Manning's *Dictionarium Saxonico et Gothico-Latinum* (1772) follow closely the methodology outlined by Hickes and Thwaites.[242] Meanwhile, as Frazier Wood has pointed out, in the 18th century there was a growing interest in the Anglo-Saxon period, which led to an increasing importance of OE in politics, culture and literature: 'In the works of early eighteenth-century philological Anglo-Saxonists, the (Old) English language becomes a synecdoche for English identity; not only the process of language acquisition but the very act of speaking narrows the conceptual divide between past and present and affirms the fundamental Anglo-Saxonness of modern-day (Old) English speakers'.[243] However, in this broad cultural setting, the scientific description and analysis of OE was no longer a primary goal. Interestingly, innovation came from continental Europe. The very area where Hickes and Thwaites had struggled, that is, the verbs, was a focal point of study for the Dutch private scholar and linguist Lambert ten Kate (1674–1731), a scion of a mercantile family whose fortune left him free to

---

[240] Elstob, *The Rudiments*, 9. [241] *Ibid.* iii.

[242] Junius, *Etymologicum Anglicanum*, ed. Lye, b2v–c1r; Lye and Manning, *Dictionarium*, g1r–g2r; Clunies Ross and Collins, *The Correspondence*, 35.

[243] Frazier Wood, *Anglo-Saxonism*, 29–30.

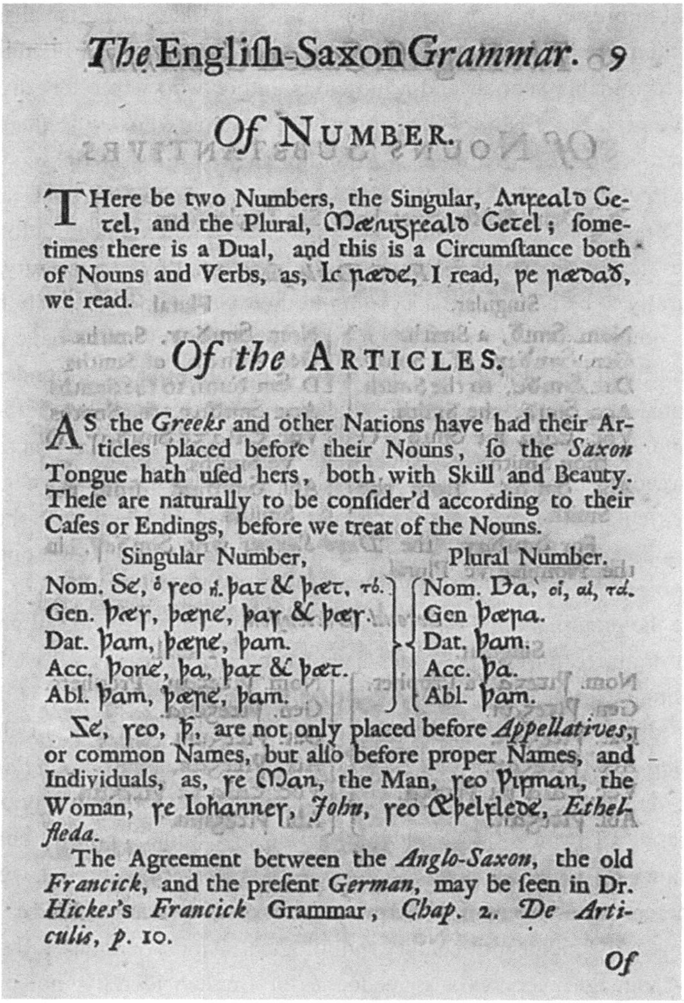

The Englilh-Saxon *Grammar.* 9

Of NUMBER.

THere be two Numbers, the Singular, Anɣealꝺ Geꞇel, and the Plural, Ɱænꞃꞅɣealꝺ Geꞇel ; fome-
times there is a Dual, aṇd this is a Circumſtance both
of Nouns and Verbs, as, Iꞔ ɣæꝺé, I read, ɣe ɣæꝺaꝺ,
we read.

Of the ARTICLES.

AS the *Greeks* and other Nations have had their Ar-
ticles placed before their Nouns, fo the *Saxon*
Tongue hath uſed hers, both with Skill and Beauty.
Theſe are naturally to be conſider'd according to their
Caſes or Endings, before we treat of the Nouns.

Singular Number,	Plural Number.
Nom. Sé, ó ɣeo ń. þaꞇ & þæꞇ, ꞇó.	Nom. Ꝺa, *oi, ai,* ꞇá.
Gen. þær, þæɲé, þaɣ & þæɲ.	Gen þæɲa.
Dat. þam, þæɲé, þam.	Dat. þam.
Acc. þoné, þa, þaꞇ & þæꞇ.	Acc. þa.
Abl. þam, þæɲé, þam.	Abl. þam.

Sé, ɣeo, þ, are not only placed before *Appellatives*,
or common Names, but alſo before proper Names, and
Individuals, as, ɣe Ɱan, the Man, ɣeo Pɣɱan, the
Woman, ɣe Iohanneɣ, *John,* ɣeo Œþelɣleꝺé, *Ethel-
fleda.*
The Agreement between the *Anglo-Saxon,* the old
Francick, and the preſent *German,* may be ſeen in Dr.
Hickes's *Francick* Grammar, *Chap.* 2. *De Arti-
culis, p.* 10.

Of

Figure 9 Elstob, *The Rudiments of Grammar,* 9

pursue his scholarly ambitions: natural philosophy and language. One of ten
Kate's major advances was the distinction between two main verb categories in
OE and other Old Germanic languages. One category he termed 'even-flowing'
verbs: these were the verbs whose stem vowel did not change in the conjugations, which ten Kate divided into two subgroups, the one following *læran*, the
other *lufian*, our modern weak 1 and weak 2 verbs. The other category consisted
of 'uneven-flowing' verbs, which changed their stem vowels: these included
what we now classify as strong verbs. For those, he designed categories
according to the number of vowel changes in the principal parts: four or three

or two, and the endings of the past participle: -en or -t(e). Each sequence of alternating vowels is then given its own sub-class: for example, ten Kate listed thirty verbs following *beodan, bead, budon, boden*; thirty-one following *bindan, band, bundon, bunden*; forty-four following *drifan, draf, drifon, drifen*; and also nine examples of weak verbs with mutated past tense forms, such as *bycgan, bohte*. Although ten Kate is still a long way away from understanding the causes of vowel gradation, his work constitutes the first attempt to establish regularity based on observations, a lesson which was noticed by Rasmus Rask (1787–1832) and Jacob Grimm (1785–1863). Despite the fact that Edward Lye was made aware of ten Kate's work in 1741,[244] it was ignored. It was Hickes's grammar that would dominate OE studies throughout the 18th century and even into the 19th.[245]

6 Transitions and Turning Points

In their attempts to periodise the history and development of OE studies, most historiographers agree that the early 19th century witnessed a turning point from traditional OE studies to 'modern' philology. Any attempts at periodisation, though, are fraught with difficulties because temporal developments are never clear-cut: the more precisely we wish to delimit a phase or period, the more difficult or impossible the argumentation becomes. Eleanor A. Adams pointed to 1834 as 'the end of the system of OE study built up by the generations of English theologians and antiquaries from Matthew Parker to George Hickes'. England had, in Adam's view, become a 'treasure house for continental scholars', whose national temperament and 'superior knowledge of all the Teutonic dialects had given them an edge over the English, who had allowed OE scholarship to slump'.[246] The idea of the second half of the 18th century as an 'ebb tide' for OE studies was certainly articulated by Adams and echoed completely, or in part, by many who came after her, including J. A. W. Bennett,[247] and particularly so by Michael Murphy, who optimistically classified the latter part of the 18th century as 'not a total wasteland for Early English philology', while emphasising the decisive importance of continental scholarship, which brought about a transition 'from the enthusiastic to the scientific in Anglo-Saxon studies in England'.[248] Whereas some focused mostly on a perceived demise of OE studies, others have taken the perspective of innovation. Writing about OE poetry, Richard Payne points to the work of Sharon Turner (1768–1847) and John Josias Conybeare (1779–1824) as

[244] Clunies Ross and Collins, *The Correspondence*, 144.

[245] Hughes, 'The Anglo-Saxon Grammars', 119–20; Harris, *A Chorus*, 24–8.

[246] Adams, *Old English Scholarship*, 110.   [247] Bennett, *The History*, 201.

[248] Murphy, 'Antiquary to Academic', 12–14.

heralding a new age in the study of OE literature.[249] Rosemary Sweet, likewise, referred to the innovation brought about by Turner, Conybeare and James Ingram, but nuances her judgement by cautioning that they 'were riding on the gathering swell of a wave which was to crest later in the Victorian period in the articulation of theories of Teutonic racial superiority'.[250] With the focus on the evolution of philological method, Haruko Momma points to John Mitchell Kemble (1807–57) as the promoter of a paradigm shift in OE studies, a change which had, according to Momma, its roots in the 18th century, when William Jones first discovered the affinity of Sanskrit with Latin and Greek.[251] Most valuable for its sophisticated approach is Allen Frantzen's section on 'The Point of the Turning Point', in which the 'turning point' itself is critically questioned. 'The idea of a "turning point"', Frantzen contends, 'is based on an attitude towards the "pastness" of the past', as seen by historiographers and philologists. Reality, as Frantzen argues, was not so clear-cut: 'Kemble, the pioneer of Germanic philology in English scholarship ... railed against papists with the vehemence of a Renaissance reformer'.[252] Nonetheless, although their motivations resembled those of their forebears, Kemble, Conybeare, Turner and others openly disapproved of earlier scholarship and actively set out to explore new routes.

To understand the turning point or transition in OE studies in the 1820s and 1830s, it is essential to review the landscape of OE studies in the 18th century, when England witnessed a 'more popular, historical and antiquarian strand of Anglo-Saxon studies and Anglo-Saxonism that developed concurrently with the philological and textual research'.[253] The language of this Anglo-Saxonism was English rather than Latin; its contributors and audience were found among the burgeoning middle classes; its media were not only printed books but also periodicals such as the *Gentleman's Magazine* and the publications of the newly re-founded Society of Antiquaries.[254] Translations of earlier Latin studies such as Edmund Gibson's translation of William Camden's *Britannia* (1695), as well as new works such as Joseph Strutt's (1749–1802) splendidly illustrated *Horda Angel-cynnan* (1775–6), inspired artists to produce images and imaginings of early medieval Britain that appealed to the neo-classical tastes of their audience. Far from being exclusionary, or male/Latin dominated, this new Anglo-Saxonism inspired participation, and the artists involved included several women such as the Swiss-Austrian painter Angelika Kauffmann, the novelist Ann Fuller and the poets and playwrights Ann Yearsley, Jane West and Joanna Baillie.[255] However, their creative engagement

---

[249] Payne, 'The Rediscovery', 155.   [250] Sweet, *Antiquaries*, 219.
[251] Momma, *From Philology to English Studies*, 60–2.   [252] Frantzen, *Desire*, 57.
[253] Frazier Wood, *Anglo-Saxonism*, 33.   [254] *Ibid*. 204.   [255] *Ibid*. 131, 187–90.

with the past did not produce an increased interest in the OE language or texts. Plans for a new edition of the biblical poems from the Junius manuscript faltered;[256] according to Thomas Warton's highly influential *History of English Poetry*, these 'religious rhapsodies' did not merit consideration.[257] Richard Payne explains that 'although the idea of OE poetry had captivated literary men in the later eighteenth century, a corresponding interest in the individual texts known in England before 1800 had not emerged'.[258] Editions of prose mostly served the prevailing antiquarian interests: Owen Manning's edition of King Alfred's will from the *Liber vitae* of the New Minster (1788) emerged from the Oxford attempts to stage the king as the university's founder;[259] Edward Rowe Mores (1730–78) added a series of OE documents, including some charter fragments, to his biography of Ælfric (1789).[260] Rather than having a focus of its own, the study of the OE language, too, became part of wider etymological debates, such as those conducted by William Drake and John Horne Tooke.[261] The most peculiar publication on OE is the radical proposal for teaching and learning the language by the philologist and Oxford graduate Samuel Henshall (1764/5–1807), better known as the inventor of the corkscrew. Published under the pseudo-Bedan motto of *rædende ic teace* [sic] 'reading I teach', Henshall argued that a daring challenger was required 'to assert that no correct ideas can be collected from the laborious exertions of a Hicks [sic], a Gibson, or a Wilkins; to affirm that their Latin interpretations are of little authority, unintelligible and delusory'.[262] Henshall's OE primer, purely based upon reading OE with Modern English interlinear glosses, met with severe criticism because of his gross translation errors and defamatory tone. It embraces the idea that OE could be understood by simple comparison with Modern English and without scholarly or scientific exploration. Henshall's work was indicative of the demise of some philological strands in England, which were beginning to be treated with contempt.[263]

Meanwhile, the study of OE flared up in different ways outside of the British borders, both in the United States of America and on the European Continent. In America, founding Fathers such as Benjamin Franklin (1705/6–90) and Thomas Jefferson (1743–1826) idealised early medieval English history and referred to it in their political discourse as part of a strategy for constructing ethnic and religious hierarchies in the ostensibly egalitarian new country. Convinced that OE ought to be taught in American universities, Jefferson composed an 'Essay on

---

[256] Sweet, *Antiquaries*, 203–5; Clunies Ross and Collins, *The Correspondence*, 29, 41–3.
[257] Sweet, *Antiquaries*, 223; Niles, *The Idea*, 194.   [258] Payne, 'The Rediscovery', 154.
[259] Keynes, 'The Cult of King Alfred', 324.
[260] Magennis and Swan, 'Ælfric Scholarship', 12.   [261] Sweet, *Antiquaries*, 225.
[262] Henshall, *The Saxon and English Languages*; see Frantzen, *Desire*, 165–6, who identified *rædende ic teace* as a phrase from Ælfric's *Grammar*.
[263] Frantzen, *Desire*, 55–6.

the Anglo-Saxon Language', containing an attempt at a grammar of OE followed by the first twelve chapters of Genesis for reading practice. The 'Essay', which drew inspiration from Elizabeth Elstob's *Rudiments of Grammar*, was never published during Jefferson's lifetime.[264] In Europe, the proliferation of OE studies in the late 18th and 19th centuries took place in northern Germany, Denmark and the Netherlands, all areas which historically identified themselves with OE in one way or another. In his 'Continental Contribution to the Study of Anglo-Saxon Writings up to and Including That of the Grimms', Eric Stanley paints a landscape dotted with minor text editions (or, rather, reprints) aimed at familiarising audiences with OE. The aims of these publications varied, from language comparison to the emphasis of a shared heritage, and they could involve prose as well as verse. In 1776, the Austrian librarian Carolus Michaeler published three poems, *The Battle of Brunanburh*, *Cædmon's Hymn* and *Durham*. Some two decades later the theologian Johann Oelrichs published the *Angelsächsische Chrestomathie* (1798), a selection of OE texts, mostly biblical, with modern German translations. According to the author, this was to prove the close relation between the languages, but also to foreground that the 'Anglo-Saxons were an ancient German nation' (see Figure 10). The *Voyages of Ohthere and Wulfstan* from the OE *Orosius*, was printed several times in both Germany and Denmark where interest in the Scandinavian north was strong.[265] In 1786 Grímur Jónsson Thorkelin received access to the *Beowulf* manuscript, of which two transcripts were completed the next year. After returning to Copenhagen in 1791, it took Thorkelin another twenty-four years to publish his edition, titled *De Danorum rebus gestis seculi III & IV. Poëma Danicum dialecto Anglo-Saxonica*. Its spurious attribution to a Danish poet, circa 1900 transcription errors and disastrous Latin translations caused an explosion of negative criticism by English and Danish philologists alike. While this reaction destroyed Thorkelin's reputation,[266] it also helped to boost the study of OE into a new age, in that Thorkelin's failure provided a challenge to a new generation of philologists.

The first three decades of the 19th century witnessed not so much a single turning point from an old to a new kind of philology but a period of transition which was characterised by parallel channels, some ending and others beginning. Some of these channels originated in England, where in 1823 Joseph Bosworth's *Elements of Anlo-Saxon Grammar* attempted (though not always successfully) to break new ground, and the field of literary history was revived in 1826 by John Josias Conybeare and his brother William (1787–1857). Their *Illustrations of Anglo-Saxon Poetry* presented the full scope of OE poetry,

---

[264] Hauer, 'Thomas Jefferson', 881, 885.   [265] Stanley 'The Continental Contribution', 54–5.

[266] Hall, 'The First Two Editions', 243, 246, who, for the first time, offers a considered assessment. Niles, *The Idea*, 204–8.

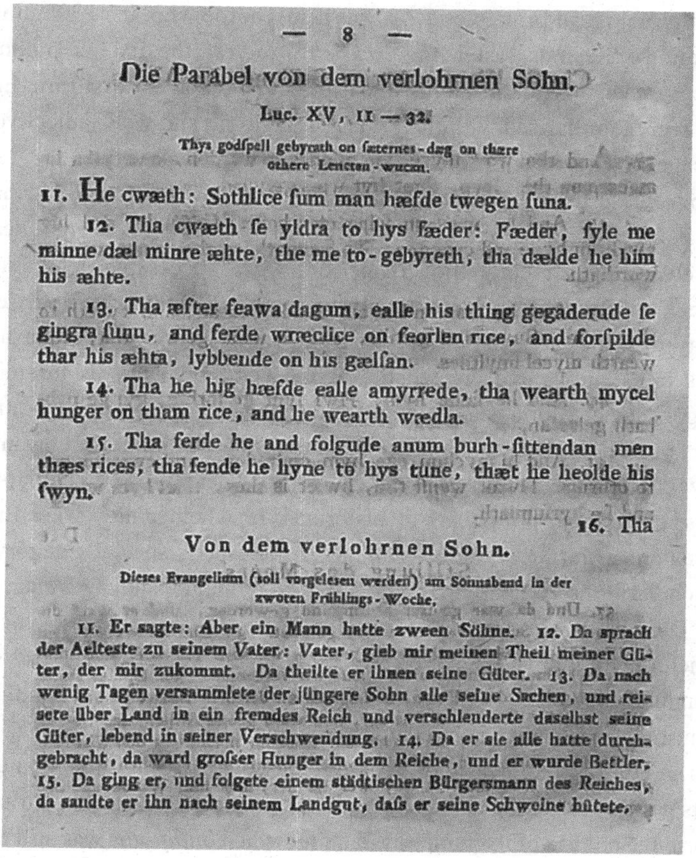

> — 8 —
>
> Die Parabel von dem verlohrnen Sohn.
>
> Luc. XV, 11 — 32.
>
> Thys godspell gebyrath on saternes-dæg on thære
> othere Lenctan-wucan.
>
> 11. He cwæth: Sothlice sum man hæfde twegen suna.
>
> 12. Tha cwæth se yldra to hys fæder: Fæder, syle me
> minne dæl minre æhte, the me to-gebyreth, tha dælde he him
> his æhte.
>
> 13. Tha æfter feawa dagum, ealle his thing gegaderude se
> gingra sunu, and ferde, wreclice on feorlen rice, and forspilde
> thar his æhta, lybbende on his gælsan.
>
> 14. Tha he hig hæfde ealle amyrrede, tha wearth mycel
> hunger on tham rice, and he wearth wædla.
>
> 15. Tha ferde he and folgude anum burh-sittendan men
> thæs rices, tha sende he hyne to hys tune, thæt he heolde his
> swyn.
>
> 16. Tha
>
> Von dem verlohrnen Sohn.
>
> Dieses Evangelium (soll vorgelesen werden) am Sonnabend in der
> zwoten Frühlings-Woche.
>
> 11. Er sagte: Aber ein Mann hatte zween Söhne. 12. Da sprach
> der Aelteste zu seinem Vater: Vater, gieb mir meinen Theil meiner Gü-
> ter, der mir zukommt. Da theilte er ihnen seine Güter. 13. Da nach
> wenig Tagen versammlete der jüngere Sohn alle seine Sachen, und rei-
> sete über Land in ein fremdes Reich und verschleuderte daselbst seine
> Güter, lebend in seiner Verschwendung. 14. Da er sie alle hatte durch-
> gebracht, da ward grosser Hunger in dem Reiche, und er wurde Bettler.
> 15. Da ging er, und folgete einem städtischen Bürgersmann des Reiches,
> da saudte er ihn nach seinem Landgut, dass er seine Schweine hütete,

Figure 10 Oelrichs, *Angelsächische Chrestomathie*, 8

including, for the first time, poems from the Exeter Book. They were also the first to articulate the basic patterns in OE alliterative verse, including the division into half lines and the function of alliteration. John Josias Conybeare was, moreover, the fourth Rawlinsonian Professor of Anglo-Saxon, a Chair funded by an endowment set up by the collector Richard Rawlinson (1690–1755), which had been filled for the first time in 1795, making OE, once again, an academic discipline. Others introduced continental philology to England. Kemble, a friend and student of Jacob Grimm, was the angry young man who preached philological revolution, and produced a corrected edition of *Beowulf* at the age of twenty-six.[267] Together with Benjamin Thorpe (1781/2–1870) they were the new faces in the field who revolutionised textual editing according to

---

[267] Momma, *From Philology to English Studies*, 68–73; Niles, *The Idea*, 220–3, 229–42.

German philological principles.[268] It was also Thorpe who, in 1830, published a translation of Rasmus Rask's *Angelsaksisk Sproglere*, the first OE grammar on empirical rather than Latin grammatical principles. For the first time English readers were familiarised with the principle of strong and weak adjectives and their usage, as well as with the system of strong and weak verbs.

Despite these new developments, it would not be right to claim that OE philology started only in the 19th century. As we have seen, a great deal had happened during the early modern period, when successive generations of scholars collected manuscripts and documents containing OE, carried out a variety of projects aimed at recording the OE lexicon, produced a flow of editions of OE texts and created the first generations of tools to study the language. Their efforts show remarkable progress, as each generation of scholars probed the language and the documents containing it for new answers to new questions, which varied according to whether these scholars were lawyers, clergymen, politicians or historians, or whether they were English, Continental, or, in the late 18th century, American. A special category were those scholars who compared OE with related Germanic languages such as Old Norse, Old High German and Gothic, and thus positioned OE in a synchronic and diachronic framework of languages, relating it to Modern English as well as its Germanic cousins. It is important to realise that all achievements in the early modern study of OE were born out of the conviction that the OE language, texts written in OE and the history of its speakers were important for the here and now. Its purpose was considered to be a moral one, in that it allowed the ancients to inform the culture of the moderns in a time when *antiquitas* was still thought to be exemplary – in religion, law, politics, the arts and language. The transition of the early 19th century marked the beginning of a change in the concept of OE philology from the study of language in a cultural context to the application of systematic principles of linguistics and textual criticism.

---

[268] Momma, *From Philology to English Studies*, 68–73; Niles, *The Idea*, 223–9.

Abbreviations

ASE	*Anglo-Saxon England*
BL	London, British Library
CCCC	Cambridge, Corpus Christi College
CUL	Cambridge, University Library
CUP	Cambridge University Press
EETS	Early English Text Society
ESTC	English Short Title Catalogue
MIP	Medieval Institute Publications
OBL	Oxford, Bodleian Library
ODNB	*Oxford Dictionary of National Biography online*
OE	Old English
OED	*Oxford English Dictionary online*
OUP	Oxford University Press
PIMS	Pontifical Institute of Medieval Studies

Bibliography

Primary Sources

Manuscripts

Cambridge, Corpus Christi College 379 (Robert Talbot's notebook)

Cambridge, Trinity College R. 9. 8. [812] (16th-century transcript of Ælfric's *Grammar*)

Cambridge, University Library, Add. 7489 (John Bale's letter to Matthew Parker)

Canterbury, Cathedral Archives, LitMS E20–1 (William Somner's *Dictionarium Saxonico-Latino-Anglicum*)

Hamburg, Staats und Universitätsbibliothek, Cod. germ. 22 (Friedrich Lindenbrog's *Glossarium Anglo-Saxonico-Latinum*)

London, British Library, Add. 4720–2 (18th-century edited copy of Franciscus Junius's *Lexicon Saxonicum*)

> Add. 18160 (preliminary version of *A Testimonie of Antiquitie*)
>
> Add. 34600 (observations on OE grammar by Abraham Wheelock and William Retchford)
>
> Add. 35333 (OE grammar by William Retchford)
>
> Cotton Nero C. iii (list of OE manuscripts and texts by John Joscelyn)
>
> Cotton Titus A. xv and xvi (Joscelyn's *Dictionarium Saxonico-Latinum*)
>
> Harley 8, 9 (Sir Simonds D'Ewes's dictionary of OE)
>
> Harley 589 (a transcript of Ælfric's *Grammar* made for Sir Simonds D'Ewes)
>
> Harley 761 (Abraham Wheelock's *Lexicon Saxonicum* with notes on OE grammar at the end)
>
> Harley 3317 (Humfrey Wanley's personal compendium of OE)
>
> Henry Davis 59 (Laurence Nowell's manuscript edition and translation of the Laws of King Alfred)

London, Lambeth Palace Library, 692 (John Joscelyn's alphabetical glossaries of OE)

London, Westminster Abbey, MS 30 (Laurence Nowell's partly abridged transcript of Ælfric's *Grammar*)

Oxford, Bodleian Library, Bodley 33 (John Parker index to John Joscelyn's grammar of OE)

> Dugdale 29 (Sir William Dugdale's dictionary of OE)

e Musaeo 161 (Gerard Langbaine's transcript of Ælfric's *Grammar*)

Fell 8–18 (William Nicolson's dictionary of northern languages)

James 42 (anonymous glossaries of OE)

Junius 2, 3 (Franciscus Junius's *Lexicon Anglo-Saxonicum*)

Junius 4, 5 (Franciscus Junius's *Etymologicum Anglicanum*)

Junius 7 (Franciscus Junius's personal copy of William Somner's *Dictionarium Saxonico-Latino-Anglicum*)

Junius 12 (Franciscus Junius's transcript of the OE *Boethius*)

Junius 15 (Franciscus Junius's transcript of the OE *Orosius*)

Junius 98 (Franciscus Junius's copy of Vulcanius, *De literis & lingua Getarum sive Gothorum*)

Marshall 78 (notes on OE and Gothic grammar written for Thomas Marshall)

Oxford, Lincoln College Library, N. 1. 7 (Parker's/Foxe's *The Gospels of the Fower Evangelistes* annotated by Franciscus Junius)

Printed Books in Chronological Order

[Parker, Matthew (1566/7)]. *A Testimonie of Antiquitie*. London: John Day.

Lambarde, William (1568). *Archaionomia, sive de priscis anglorum legibus libri*. London: John Day.

Flacius Illyricus, Matthias (1571). *Otfridi Evangeliorum liber*. Basel: Heinrich Petri.

[Foxe, John] (1571). *The Gospels of the Fower Evangelistes*. London: John Day.

Parker, Matthew (1574). *Ælfredi Regis Res Gestæ*. London: John Day.

Vulcanius, Bonaventura (1597). *De literis et lingua Getarum sive Gothorum*. Leiden: Franciscus Raphelengius.

Camden, William (1605). *Remaines of a Greater Worke, Concerning Britaine*. London: G. E. for Simon Waterson.

Verstegan, Richard (1605). *A Restitution of Decayed Intelligence: In Antiquities*. Antwerp: Robert Bruney.

Freher, Marquard (1610). *Decalogi orationis symboli Saxonica versio vetustissima*. Heidelberg: Gotthard Voegelin.

L'Isle, William (1623). *A Saxon Treatise Concerning the Old and New Testament*. London: John Haviland.

Spelman, Henry (1639). *Concilia, decreta, leges, constitutiones*. London: Roger Badger.

Spelman, John (1640). *Psalterium Davidis Latino–Saxonicum vetus*. London: Roger Badger.

Wheelock, Abraham (1643). *Historiæ ecclesiasticæ gentis Anglorum libri V.* Cambridge: Roger Daniel.

Wheelock, Abraham (1644). *Archaionomia, Sive de priscis anglorum legibus libri.* Cambridge: Roger Daniel.

Casaubon, Meric (1650). *De Quatuor Linguis Commentationis Pars Prior.* London: James Flesher.

Twysden, Roger (1652), *Historiæ Anglicanæ Scriptores X.* London: James Flesher.

Junius, Franciscus (1655). *Observationes in Willerami abbatis Francicam paraphrasis Cantici Canticorum.* Amsterdam: Christoffel Cunrad.

Junius, Franciscus (1655). *Cædmonis monachi paraphrasis poetica Genesios.* Amsterdam: Christoffel Cunrad.

Somner, William (1659), *Dictionarium Saxonico-Latino-Anglicum.* Oxford: William Hall.

Junius, Franciscus, and Thomas Marshall (1665), *Quatuor D.N.J.C. evangeliorum versiones perantiquæ duæ.* Dordrecht: Van Esch.

Junius, Franciscus (1665). *Gothicum Glossarium.* Dordrecht: Van Esch.

Hickes, George (1689). *Institutiones Grammaticæ.* Oxford: Sheldonian Press.

Gibson, Edmund (1692). *Chronicon Saxonicum ex MSS Codicibus.* Oxford: Sheldonian Press.

Gibson, Edmund (1695). *Camden's Britannia Newly Translated into English, with Large Additions and Improvements.* London: F. Collins.

Nicolson, William (1696). *The English Historical Library.* London: Swall and Child.

Rawlinson, Christopher (1698). *A. Manl. Sever. Boethii Consolationis Philosophiæ libri V.* Oxford: Sheldonian Press.

Thwaites, Edward (1698). *Heptateuchus, Liber Job, et Evangelium Nicodemi.* Oxford: Sheldonian Press.

Benson, Thomas (1701). *Vocabularium Anglo-Saxonicum.* Oxford: Sheldonian Press.

Hickes, George (1703–5). *Linguarum vett. Septentrionalium thesaurus grammatico-criticus & archæologicus.* Oxford: Sheldonian Press.

Wanley, Humfrey (1705). *Librorum vett. Septentrionalium, qui in Angliæ Biblioth. Extant, Catalogus.* Oxford: Sheldonian Press.

Elstob, Elizabeth (1709). *An English-Saxon Homily on the Birth-Day of St. Gregory.* London: William Bowyer.

Thwaites, Edward (1711). *Grammatica Anglo-Saxonica.* Oxford: Sheldonian Press.

Elstob, Elizabeth (1715). *The Rudiments of Grammar for the English-Saxon Tongue.* London: William Bowyer.

Hearne, Thomas (1720). *Textus Roffensis.* Oxford: Sheldonian Press.

Wilkins, David (1721). *Leges Anglo-Saxonicæ Ecclesiasticæ et Civiles.* London: William Bowyer.

Smith, John (1722). *Historiæ Ecclesiasticæ Gentis Anglorum Libri quinque.* Cambridge: Cambridge University Press.

Ten Kate, Lambert (1723). *Aenleiding tot de kennisse van het verhevene deel der Nederduitsche sprake.* Amsterdam: Wetstein.

Hearne, Thomas (1726). *Johannis, confratris et monachi Glastoniensis, Chronica sive historia de rebus Glastoniensibus.* Oxford: Sheldonian Press.

Junius, Franciscus (1743). *Etymologicum Anglicanum,* ed. by Edward Lye. Oxford: Sheldonian Press.

Lye, Edward, and Owen Manning (1772). *Dictionarium Saxonico et Gothico-Latinum.* London: Edmund Allen.

Barrington, Daines (1773). *Orosius: the Anglo-Saxon Version.* London: William Bowyer.

Strutt, Joseph (1775). *Horda Angel-cynnan: or A Compleat View of the Manners, Customs, Arms, Habits, &c. of the Inhabitants of England.* London: Sold by Benjamin White.

Michaeler, Carolus (1776). *Tabulæ parallelæ antiquissimarum Teutonicæ linguæ dialectorum.* Innsbruck: Wagner.

Drake, William (1779). 'A Letter to the Secretary, on the Origins of the English Language'. *Archaeologia* 5: 306–17, 379–89.

Tooke, John Horne (1786). *The Diversions of Purley.* London: J. Johnson.

Manning, Owen (1788). *The Will of King Alfred.* Oxford: Clarendon Press.

Mores, Edward Rowe (1789). *De Ælfrico Dorobernensi Archiepiscopo commentarius.* London: Charles Clark.

Henshall, Samuel (1798). *The Saxon and English Languages.* London: Printed for the Author.

Oelrichs, Johann (1798). *Angelsächische Chrestomathie.* Hamburg: Hofmann.

Ingram, James (1807). *An Inaugural Lecture of the Utility of Anglo-Saxon.* Oxford: Oxford University Press.

Thorkelin, Grímur Jónsson (1815). *De Danorum rebus gestis secul. III et IV.* Copenhagen: Rangel.

Rask, Rasmus (1817). *Angelsaksisk Sproglaere.* Stockholm: Hedman.

Bosworth, Joseph (1823). *The Elements of Anglo-Saxon Grammar.* London: Harding, Mayor and Lepard.

Warton, Thomas (1824). *The History of English Poetry.* London: J. Dodsley *et al.*

Conybeare, John Josias, and William Conybeare (1826). *Illustrations of Anglo-Saxon Poetry.* London: Harding and Lepard.

Thorpe, Benjamin (1830). *A Grammar of the Anglo-Saxon Tongue, with a Praxis by Erasmus Rask.* Copenhagen: S. L. Møller.

Kemble, John Mitchel (1833). *The Anglo-Saxon Poems of Beowulf.* London: Pickering.

Petherham, John (1840). *An Historical Sketch of the Progress and Present State of Anglo-Saxon Literature in England.* London: Edward Lumley.

White, Robert Meadows (1852). *The Ormulum, Now First Edited from the Original Manuscript in the Bodleian Library, with Notes and a Glossary.* Oxford: Oxford University Press.

Secondary Sources

Adams, E. N. (1917). *Old English Scholarship from 1566–1800.* New Haven: Yale University Press; repr. (1970). Hamden, CT: Archon Books.

Bankert, D. A. (2012). 'Oxford, Bodleian Library, MS Rawlinson C.887: An Unpublished Seventeenth-Century Anglo-Saxon Glossary by Nathaniel Spinckes'. *The Library* 13: 400–22.

Bately, J. (1993). 'John Joscelyn and the Laws of the Anglo-Saxon Kings'. In M. Korhammer, K. Reichl and H. Sauer, eds. *Words, Texts and Manuscripts: Studies in Anglo-Saxon Culture Presented to Helmut Gneuss on the Occasion of his 65th Birthday.* Cambridge: D. S. Brewer, 435–66.

Baugh, A. C., and T. Cable (2013). *A History of the English Language,* sixth ed. Abingdon: Routledge.

Bennett, J. A. W. (1938). 'The History of Old English and Old Norse Studies in England from the Time of Francis Junius till the End of the Eighteenth Century'. PhD diss., Merton College, Oxford.

Berkhout, C. T. (2021). 'Laurence Nowell and the Old English Bede'. In L. Brady, ed., *Old English Tradition: Essays in Honor of J. R. Hall.* Tempe: ACMRS, 261–74.

(2000). 'William Lambarde and Old English'. *Notes and Queries* 245: 415–20.

(1998). 'Laurence Nowell (1530–ca. 1570)'. In H. Damico, D. Fennema and K. Lenz, eds., *Medieval Scholarship: Biographical Studies on the Formation of a Discipline. Volume 2: Literature and Philology.* New York: Garland, 3–16.

(1985). 'The Pedigree of Laurence Nowell the Antiquary'. *English Language Notes* 23: 15–26.

Brackmann, R. (2023). *Old English Scholarship in the Seventeenth Century: Medievalism and National Crisis,* Medievalism 23. Cambridge: D. S. Brewer.

(2012). *The Elizabethan Invention of Anglo-Saxon England: Laurence Nowell, William Lambarde, and the Study of Old English.* Cambridge: D. S. Brewer.

(2010). 'Laurence Nowell's Edition and Translation of the Laws of Alfred'. *Heroic Age* 14: n.p. www.heroicage.org/issues/14.brackmann.php.

Bremmer, R. H. (2008). '"Mine Is Bigger Than Yours": The Anglo-Saxon Collections of Johannes de Laet (1581–1649) and Sir Simonds D'Ewes (1602–50)'. In T. N. Hall and D. Scragg, eds., *Anglo-Saxon Books and Their Readers: Essays in Celebration of Helmut Gneuss's Handlist of Anglo-Saxon Manuscripts*. Kalamazoo, MI: MedilP, 136–74.

(1998). 'The Correspondence of Johannes de Laet (1581–1649) as a Mirror of His Life'. *Lias* 25: 139–64.

Bremmer, R. H. and K. Dekker (2006). *Manuscripts in the Low Countries*, Anglo-Saxon Manuscripts in Microfiche Facsimile 13. Tempe: ACMRS.

Bromwich, J. (1962). 'The First Book Printed in Anglo-Saxon Types'. *Transactions of the Cambridge Bibliographical Society* 3: 265–91.

Buckalew, R. E. (1982). 'Nowell, Lambarde and Leland: The Significance of Laurence Nowell's Transcript of Ælfric's Grammar and Glossary'. In C. Berkhout and M. McC Gatch, eds., *Anglo-Saxon Scholarship, The First Three Centuries*. Boston, MA: G. K. Hall & Co., 19–50.

(1978). 'Leland's Transcript of Ælfric's Glossary'. *ASE* 8: 149–64.

Cain, C. M. (2010). 'George Hickes and the "Invention" of the Old English Dialects'. *Review of English Studies* 61, no. 252: 729–48.

Carley, J. P. (2006). 'The Dispersal of the Monastic Libraries and the Salvaging of the Spoils'. In E. Leedham-Green and T. Webber, eds., *The Cambridge History of Libraries in Britain and Ireland, vol. 1: To 1640*. Cambridge: CUP, 265–91.

Clement, R. W. (1997). 'The Beginnings of Printing in Anglo-Saxon, 1565–1630'. *Papers of the Bibliographical Society of America* 91.2: 192–244.

Clunies Ross, M. and A. J. Collins (2004). *The Correspondence of Edward Lye*. Toronto: PIMS.

Considine, J. (2008). *Dictionaries in Early Modern Europe: Lexicography and the Making of Heritage*. Cambridge: CUP.

Dekker, K. (2022). *Anglo-Saxon, Norse and Celtic in the Work of Franciscus Junius*, E. C. Quiggin Memorial Lectures 22. Cambridge: Department of Anglo-Saxon, Norse and Celtic.

(2008). 'Reading the Anglo-Saxon Gospels in the Sixteenth and Seventeenth Centuries'. In T. N. Hall and D. Scragg, eds., *Anglo-Saxon Books and Their Readers: Papers in Celebration of Helmut Gneuss's Handlist of Anglo-Saxon Manuscripts*. Kalamazoo: MIP, 68–93.

(2000). '"That Most Elaborate One of Francis Junius": An Investigation of Francis Junius's Manuscript Old English Dictionary'. In T. Graham, ed.,

The Recovery of Old English: Anglo-Saxon Studies in the Sixteenth and Seventeenth Centuries. Kalamazoo: MIP, 301–43.

(2000). 'Francis Junius (1591–1677): Copyist or Editor?'. *ASE* 29: 279–96.

(1999). *The Origins of Old Germanic Studies in the Low Countries*. Leiden: Brill.

DOEC = Healey, A. DiPaolo, with J. P. Wilkin and X. Xiang (2009). *Dictionary of Old English Web Corpus*, Toronto: Dictionary of Old English Project.

Fletcher, R. A. (2021). 'Pushing the Boundary: The Periodisation Problem in Dictionaries of Old English', PhD diss., University of Glasgow.

(2018). '"Most Active and Effectual Assistance" in the Correspondence of Sir William Dugdale and William Somner'. *Amsterdamer Beiträge zur älteren Germanistik* 78: 166–84.

(2017). 'William Somner's *Dictionarium Saxonico-Latino-Anglicum*: Method, Function and Legacy', MPhil. diss., University of Glasgow.

Frantzen, A. J. (1990). *Desire for Origins: New Language, Old English, and Teaching the Tradition*. New Brunswick: Rutgers University Press.

Frantzen, A. J. and J. D. Niles (1997). 'Introduction: Anglo-Saxonism'. In A. J. Frantzen and J. D. Niles, eds., *Anglo-Saxonism and the Construction of Social Identity*. Gainesville: Florida University Press, 1–14.

Franzen, C. (1991). *The Tremulous Hand of Worcester: A Study of Old English in the Thirteenth Century*. Oxford: Clarendon Press.

Frazier Wood, D. (2020). *Anglo-Saxonism and the Idea of Englishness in Eighteenth-Century Britain*. Woodbridge: The Boydell Press.

Gatch, M. McC. (1998). 'Humfrey Wanley (1672–1726)'. In H. Damico, D. Fennema and K. Lenz, eds., *Medieval Scholarship: Biographical Studies on the Formation of a Discipline, vol. 2: Literature and Philology*. New York: Garland, 45–57.

Gneuss, H. (1996). *English Language Scholarship: A Survey and Bibliography from the Beginnings to the End of the Nineteenth Century*. Binghamton, NY: Medieval and Renaissance Texts and Studies.

(1993). 'Der älteste Katalog der angelsächsischen Handschriften und seine Nachfolger'. In K. R. Grinda and C.-D. Wetzel, eds., *Anglo-Saxonica. Festschrift für Hans Schabram zum 65. Geburtstag*. Munich: Wilhelm Finck, 91–106; repr. (1996). Books and Libraries in Early England. Aldershot: Ashgate, nr. X.

(1990). 'The Study of Language in Anglo-Saxon England'. *Bulletin of the John Rylands University Library of Manchester* 72: 3–32.

Godden, M. (1977). 'Old English'. In A. G. Rigg, ed., *Editing Medieval Texts English French, and Latin Written in England*. New York: Garland, 9–33.

Goepp, P. H. (1949). 'Verstegan's "Most Ancient Saxon Words"'. In T. A. Kirby and H. B. Woolf, eds., *Philologica: The Malone Anniversary Studies*. Baltimore, MD: Johns Hopkins Press, 249–55.

Grafton, A. (2017). 'Matthew Parker: The Book as Archive'. *History of Humanities* 2: 15–50.

Graham, T. (2022). 'Abraham Wheelock, Agent of Anglicanism, and the Deployment of Old English Texts in the 1643 Edition of Bede's *Ecclesiastical History of the English People*'. In J. Fay, R. Stephenson and R. R. Trilling, eds., *Textual Identities in Early Medieval England: Essays in Honour of Katherine O'Brien O'Keeffe*. Cambridge: D. S. Brewer, 170–204.

(2021). *Elizabeth Elstob's 'English-Saxon Homily on the Birth-Day of St. Gregory'*. Troy, AL: Witan Publishing.

(2020). 'Old English and Old Norse Studies to the Eighteenth Century'. In J. Parker and C. Wagner, eds., *The Oxford Handbook of Victorian Medievalism*. Oxford: Oxford University Press, 24–52.

(2020). 'The Early Modern Afterlife of Exeter's Anglo-Saxon Manuscripts'. In E. J. Christie, ed., *The Wisdom of Exeter: Anglo-Saxon Studies in Honor of Patrick W. Conner*. Kalamazoo: MIP, 77–130.

(2014). 'William Elstob's Planned Edition of the Anglo-Saxon Laws: A Remnant in the Takamiya Collection'. In S. Horobin and L. R. Mooney, eds., *Middle English Texts in Translation: A Festschrift Dedicated to Toshiyuki Takamiya on his 70th Birthday*. Woodbridge: York Medieval Press, 268–96.

(2006). 'Matthew Parker's Manuscripts: An Elizabethan Library and Its Use'. In E. Leedham-Green and T. Webber, eds., *The Cambridge History of Libraries in Britain and Ireland, vol. 1: To 1640*. Cambridge: CUP, 322–44.

(2001). 'Anglo-Saxon Studies: Sixteenth to Eighteenth Centuries'. In P. Pulsiano and E. Treharne, eds., *A Companion to Anglo-Saxon Literature*. Oxford: Blackwell, 415–33.

(2000). 'John Joscelyn, Pioneer of Old English Lexicography'. In T. Graham, ed., *The Recovery of Old English: Anglo-Saxon Studies in the Sixteenth and Seventeenth Centuries*. Kalamazoo: MIP, 83–140.

(2000). 'Early Modern Users of Claudius B.iv: Robert Talbot and William L'Isle'. In R. Barnhouse and B. C. Withers, eds., *The Old English Hexateuch: Aspects and Approaches*, Kalamazoo: MIP, 271–313.

(1997). 'Robert Talbot's "Old Saxonice Bede": Cambridge University Library, MS Kk.3.18 and the "Alphabetum Norwagicum" of British Library, Cotton MSS, Domitian A. IX'. In J. P. Carley and C. G. C. Tite, eds., *Books and Collectors 1200–1700: Essays Presented to Andrew Watson*. London: British Library, 295–316.

(1997). 'The Beginnings of Old English Studies: Evidence from the Manuscripts of Matthew Parker'. In S. Sato, ed., *Back to the Manuscripts: Papers from the Symposium 'The Integrated Approach to Manuscript Studies: A New Horizon'*. Tokyo: The Centre for Medieval English Studies, 29–50.

(1996). 'The Earliest Old English Word-List from Tudor England'. *Medieval English Studies Newsletter* 35: 4–7.

Graham, T. and A. G. Watson (1998). *The Recovery of the Past in Early Elizabethan England: Documents by John Bale and John Joscelyn from the Circle of Matthew Parker*. Cambridge: CUL.

Gretsch, M. (1999). 'Elizabeth Elstob: A Scholar's Fight for Anglo-Saxon Studies'. *Anglia* 117: 163–200 and 481–524.

Hall, J. R. (1994). 'The First Two Editions of *Beowulf*: Thorkelin's (1815) and Kemble's (1833)'. In D. G. Scragg and P. E. Szarmach, eds., *The Editing of Old English: Papers from the 1990 Manchester Conference*. Cambridge: D. S. Brewer, 239–50.

Hamilton, A. (2017). 'The Qur'an as Chrestomathy in Early Modern Europe'. In J. Loop, A. Hamilton and C. Burnett, eds., *The Teaching and Learning of Arabic in Early Modern Europe*. Leiden: Brill, 213–29.

Hamilton, D. (1999). 'Richard Verstegan's A Restitution of Decayed Intelligence (1605): A Catholic Antiquarian Reply to John Foxe, Thomas Cooper and Jean Bodin'. *Prose Studies* 22: 1–38.

Harris, R. (1992). *A Chorus of Grammars: The Correspondence of George Hickes and His Collaborators on the Thesaurus Linguarum Septentrionalium*. Toronto: PIMS.

Hetherington, M. S. (1980). *The Beginnings of Old English Lexicography*. Spicewood: private publication.

Hollis, D. (2015). 'On the Margins of Scholarship: The Letters of Elizabeth Elstob to George Ballard, 1735–1753'. *Lias* 42: 167–268.

Hüllen, W. (1999). *English Dictionaries: The Topical Tradition*. Oxford: OUP.

Kelemen, E. (2006). 'More Evidence for the Date of *A Testimonie of Antiquitie*'. *The Library* 7: 361–76.

Ker, N. R. (1976). 'A Supplement to *Catalogue of Manuscripts Containing Anglo-Saxon*'. *ASE* 5: 120–31.

(1964). *Medieval Libraries of Great Britain: A List of Surviving Books*, 2nd edition. London: Royal Historical Society.

(1957). *Catalogue of Manuscripts Containing Anglo-Saxon*. Oxford: OUP.

Keynes, S. (1999). 'The Cult of King Alfred the Great'. *ASE* 28: 225–356.

Lancashire, I. (2018). *Lexicons of Early Modern English.* Toronto: University of Toronto Press, 2018. http://leme.library.utoronto.ca

Lerer, S. (2001). 'The Anglo-Saxon Pindar: Old English Scholarship and Augustan Criticism in George Hickes's *Thesaurus'. Modern Philology* 99: 26–65.

Levine, J. M. (1987). *Humanism and History: Origins of Modern English Historiography.* Ithaca: Cornell University Press.

Lewis, C. T. and C. Short (1879). *A Latin Dictionary.* Oxford: Clarendon Press.

Liebermann, F. (1903–16). *Die Gesetze der Angelsachsen.* 3 vols. Halle: Niemeyer.

Liuzza, R. M. (1994). *The Old English Version of the Gospels,* EETS OS 304. Oxford: OUP.

Lowe, K. A. (2000). '"The Oracle of His Countrey"? William Somner, *Gavelkind,* and Lexicography in the Seventeenth and Eighteenth Centuries'. In T. Graham, ed., *The Recovery of Old English: Anglo-Saxon Studies in the Seventeenth and Eighteenth Centuries.* Kalamazoo: MIP, 281–300.

(1999). 'William Somner and the Editing of Old English Charters'. *Neophilologus* 83: 291–97.

Lucas, P. J. (2016). 'The Earliest Modern Anglo-Saxon Grammar: Sir Henry Spelman, Abraham Wheelock and William Retchford'. *ASE* 45: 397–417.

(2006). 'Abraham Wheelock and the Presentation of Anglo-Saxon: From Manuscript to Print'. In A. N. Doane and K. Wolf, eds., *Beatus Vir: Studies in Early English and Norse Manuscripts in Memory of Phillip Pulsiano.* Tempe, AZ: ACMRS, 383–439.

(1999). 'Parker, Lambarde and the Provision of Special Sorts for Printing Anglo-Saxon in the Sixteenth Century'. *Journal of the Printing Historical Society* 28: 41–69.

(1997). 'Franciscus Junius and the Versification of *Judith'.* In P. E. Szarmach and J. T. Rosenthal, eds., *The Preservation and Transmission of Anglo-Saxon Culture.* Kalamazoo: MIP, 369–404.

(1997). 'Junius, his Printers and His Types: An Interim Report'. In R. H., Bremmer Jr, ed., *Francis Junius and His Circle.* Amsterdam: Rodopi, 177–235.

(1997). 'A Testimonye of Verye Ancient Tyme? Some Manuscript Models for the Parkerian Anglo-Saxon Type-Designs'. In P. R. Robinson and R. Zim, eds., *Of the Making of Books: Medieval Manuscripts, Their Scribes and Readers.* Aldershot: Scolar Press, 147–88.

(1995). 'The Metrical Epilogue to the Alfredian Pastoral Care: a Postscript from Junius'. *ASE* 24: 43–50.

Lutz, A. (2000). 'The Study of the Anglo-Saxon Chronicle in the Seventeenth Century and the Establishment of Old English Studies in the Universities'. In T. Graham, ed., *The Recovery of Old English: Anglo-Saxon Studies in the Sixteenth and Seventeenth Centuries*. Kalamazoo: MIP, 1–82.

(1988). 'Zur Entstehungsgeschichte von William Somners *Dictionarium Saxonico-Latino-Anglicum*'. *Anglia* 106: 1–25.

(1982). 'Das Studium der Angelsächsischen Chronik im 16. Jahrhundert: Nowell und Joscelyn'. *Anglia* 100: 301–56.

(1981). *Die Version G der angelsächsischen Chronik: Rekonstruktion und Edition*. Munich: Fink.

Magennis, H. and M. Swan (2009). 'Ælfric Scholarship'. In H. Magennis and M. Swan, eds., *A Companion to Ælfric*. Leiden: Brill.

Mann, N. (1996). 'The Origins of Humanism'. In J. Kraye, ed., *The Cambridge Companion to Renaissance Humanism*. Cambridge: CUP, 1–19.

Marckwardt, Albert H., ed. (1952). *Laurence Nowell's Vocabularium Saxonicum*. Ann Arbor: University of Michigan Press.

McCabe, S. (2010). 'Anglo-Saxon Poetics in the *Linguarum Veterum Septentrionalium Thesaurus Grammatico-Criticus et Archælogicus* of George Hickes: A Translation, Analysis, and Contextualization'. PhD diss., University of New Mexico.

Menzer, M. (2004). 'Ælfric's English Grammar'. *Journal of English and Germanic Philology* 103: 106–24.

Momma, H. (2013). *From Philology to English Studies: Language and Culture in the Nineteenth Century*. Cambridge: CUP.

Murphy, M. A. (1982). 'Antiquary to Academic: The Progress of Anglo-Saxon Scholarship'. In C. T. Berkhout and M. McC. Gatch, eds., *Anglo-Saxon Scholarship: The First Three Centuries*. Boston: G. K. Hall, 1–17.

(1967). 'Abraham Wheloc's Edition of Bede's History in Old English'. *Studia Neophilologica* 39: 46–59.

Niles, J. D. (2015). *The Idea of Anglo-Saxon England 1066–1901: Remembering, Forgetting, Deciphering and Renewing the Past*. Malden: Wiley Blackwell.

Page, R. I. (1993). *Matthew Parker and His Books*. Kalamazoo: MIP.

(1981). 'The Parker Register and Matthew Parker's Anglo-Saxon Manuscripts'. *Transactions of the Cambridge Bibliographical Society* 8.1: 1–17.

Parkes, M. (1997). 'Archaizing Hands in English Manuscripts'. In J. P. Carley and C. G. C. Tite, eds., *Books and Collectors 1200–1700*. London: British Library, 101–41.

Payne, R. C. (1982). 'The Rediscovery of Old English Poetry in the English Literary Tradition'. In C. T. Berkhout and M. McC. Gatch, eds., *Anglo-Saxon Scholarship: The First Three Centuries*. Boston: G. K. Hall, 149–66.

Plumer, D. C. (2000). 'The Construction of Structure in the Earliest Editions of Old English Poetry'. In T. Graham, ed., *The Recovery of Old English: Anglo-Saxon Studies in the Sixteenth and Seventeenth Centuries*. Kalamazoo: MIP, 243–79.

Porck, T. (2024). 'Newly Discovered Pieces of an Old English Glossed Psalter: The Alkmaar Fragments of the N-Psalter'. *ASE* (forthcoming).

Prescott, A. (1997). '"Their Present Miserable State of Cremation": The Restoration of the Cotton Library'. In C. J. Wright, ed., *Sir Robert Cotton as Collector: Essays on an Early Stuart Courtier and His Legacy*. London: British Library, 391–454.

Rudolf, W. (2023). 'Old English Lexicography in Northern Germany 1650–1730: The Manuscript Evidence'. In R. Bauer, C. Elsweiler, U. Krischke and K. Majewski, eds., *Travelling Texts – Texts Travelling: A Gedenkschrift for Hans Sauer*. Munich: UTZ, 2–44.

Rudolf, W. and S. Pelle (2021). 'Friedrich Lindenbrog's Old English Glossaries Rediscovered'. *Anglia* 139: 617–72.

Sharpe, K. (1979). *Sir Robert Cotton 1586–1631: History and Politics in Early Modern England*. Oxford: OUP.

Sisam, K. (1925). 'The Authenticity of Certain Texts in Lambarde's "Archaionomia" 1568'. *Modern Language Review* 20: 253–69; repr. (1953). *Studies in the History of Old English Literature*: Oxford: Clarendon Press, 232–58.

Skeat, W. W. (1871). *The Gospel according to Saint Mark in Anglo-Saxon and Northumbrian Versions*. Cambridge: CUP.

Stanley, E. G. (1997). 'Sources of Francis Junius' Learning as Revealed in the Junius Manuscripts in the Bodleian Library'. In R. H. Bremmer Jr., ed., *Francis Junius and His Circle*. Amsterdam: Rodopi, 159–76.

(1987). 'The Continental Contribution to the Study of Anglo-Saxon Writings up to and Including That of the Grimms'. In E. G. Stanley, ed., *A Collection of Papers with Emphasis on Old English Literature*. Toronto: PIMS, 49–74.

Summit, J. (2008). *Memory's Library: Medieval Books in Early Modern England*. Chicago: University of Chicago Press.

Sutherland, K. (1998). 'Elizabeth Elstob (1683–1756)', In H. Damico, D. Fennema and K. Lenz, eds., *Medieval Scholarship: Biographical Studies on the Formation of a Discipline, vol. 2: Literature and Philology*. New York: Garland, 59–73.

(1994). 'Editing for a New Century: Elizabeth Elstob's Anglo-Saxon Manifesto and Ælfric's St. Gregory Homily'. In D. G. Scragg and P. E. Szarmach, eds., *The Editing of Old English: Papers from the 1990 Manchester Conference.* Cambridge: D. S. Brewer, 213–37.

Sweet, R. (2004). *Antiquaries: The Discovery of the Past in Eighteenth-Century Britain.* London: Hambledon.

Tite, C. G. C. (2003). *The Early Records of Sir Robert Cotton's Library: Formation, Cataloguing, Use.* London: British Library.

Treharne, E. (2001). 'English in the Post-Conquest Period'. In P. Pulsiano and E. Treharne, eds., *A Companion to Anglo-Saxon Literature.* Oxford: Blackwell, 403–14.

Van Romburgh, S. G. (2016). 'How to Make the Past Age Present: Some of Ole Worm's and Francis Junius' Humanist Efforts'. In A. Molinari and M. Dallapiazza, eds., *Mittelalterphilologien heute: Eine Standortbestimmung. Band 1: Die germanischen Philologien.* Würzburg: Königshausen & Neumann, 157–72.

(2004). *'For My Worthy Freind Mr Franciscus Junius': An Edition of the Correspondence of Francis Junius F. F. (1591–1677).* Leiden: Brill.

Waite, G. (2021). 'John Smith's 1722 Edition of Bede's *Historia Ecclesiastica* and the Burnt British Library Cotton MS Otho B XI'. *Parergon* 38: 129–61.

Wilton, D. (2020). 'What Do We Mean by Anglo-Saxon? Pre-Conquest to the Present'. *The Journal of English and Germanic Philology* 119: 425–54.

Wormald, P. (1999). *The Making of English Law: King Alfred to the Twelfth Century.* Oxford: Blackwell.

(1997). 'The Lambarde Problem: Eighty Years On'. In J. Roberts, J. L. Nelson and M. Godden, eds., *Alfred the Wise: Studies in Honour of Janet Bately.* Cambridge: D. S. Brewer, 237–75.

Wright, C. E. (1958). 'The Dispersal of Libraries in the Sixteenth Century'. In F. Wormald and C. E. Wright, eds., *The English Library before 1700.* London: Athlone Press, 148–75.

(1951). 'The Dispersal of the Monastic Libraries and the Beginnings of Anglo-Saxon Studies: Matthew Parker and His Circle – A Preliminary Study'. *Transactions of the Cambridge Bibliographical Society* 1.3: 208–37.

Wright, C. J., ed. (1997). *Sir Robert Cotton as Collector: Essays on an Early Stuart Courtier and His Legacy.* London: British Library.

Zupitza, J., ed. (1880). *Ælfrics Grammatik und Glossar. Text und Varianten;* repr. (1966) with an introduction by Helmut Gneuss. Berlin: Weidmann.

Acknowledgements

This Element stands on the shoulders of many. It owes a tremendous debt of gratitude to Winfried Rudolf and Emily Thornbury as ever-kind and patient editors of *Cambridge Elements*, and, particularly, to the two anonymous reviewers whose meticulous corrections, detailed advice and constructive criticism offered far more than I deserved. Last but never least, Christine's support has been invaluable. The history of OE studies from its early modern beginnings up to the start of the nineteenth century is a rich and vibrant topic, as many colleagues, senior and junior, have abundantly demonstrated in their excellent work. For lack of space, full credit to all of their books and articles cannot be given here. This *Element* is dedicated to them and is intended to kindle a fire in future generations that will create a burning interest in all of their works.

Cambridge Elements ☰

England in the Early Medieval World

Megan Cavell
University of Birmingham

Megan Cavell is Associate Professor in medieval English literature at the University of Birmingham. She works on a wide range of topics in medieval literary studies, from Old and early Middle English and Latin languages and literature to riddling, gender and animal studies. Her previous publications include *Weaving Words and Binding Bodies: The Poetics of Human Experience in Old English Literature* (2016), *Riddles at Work in the Early Medieval Tradition: Words, Ideas, Interactions* (co-edited with Jennifer Neville, 2020), and *The Medieval Bestiary in England: Texts and Translations of the Old and Middle English Physiologus* (2022).

Rory Naismith
University of Cambridge

Rory Naismith is Professor of Early Medieval English History in the Department of Anglo-Saxon, Norse and Celtic at the University of Cambridge, and a Fellow of Corpus Christi College, Cambridge. Also a Fellow of the Royal Historical Society, he is the author of *Early Medieval Britain 500–1000* (Cambridge University Press, 2021), *Citadel of the Saxons: The Rise of Early London* (2018), *Medieval European Coinage, with a Catalogue of the Coins in the Fitzwilliam Museum, Cambridge, 8: Britain and Ireland c. 400–1066* (Cambridge University Press, 2017) and *Money and Power in Anglo-Saxon England: The Southern English Kingdoms 757–865* (Cambridge University Press, 2012, which won the 2013 International Society of Anglo-Saxonists First Book Prize).

Winfried Rudolf
University of Göttingen

Winfried Rudolf is Chair of Medieval English Language and Literature in the University of Göttingen (Germany). Recent publications include *Childhood and Adolescence in Anglo-Saxon Literary Culture* (with Susan E. Irvine, 2018). He has published widely on homiletic literature in early England and is currently principal investigator of the ERC-Project ECHOE–Electronic Corpus of Anonymous Homilies in Old English.

Emily V. Thornbury
Yale University

Emily V. Thornbury is Associate Professor of English at Yale University. She studies the literature and art of early England, with a particular emphasis on English and Latin poetry. Her publications include *Becoming a Poet in Anglo-Saxon England* (Cambridge, 2014), and, co-edited with Rebecca Stephenson, *Latinity and Identity in Anglo-Saxon Literature* (2016). She is currently working on a monograph called *The Virtue of Ornament*, about pre-Conquest theories of aesthetic value.

About the Series

Elements in England in the Early Medieval World takes an innovative, interdisciplinary view of the culture, history, literature, archaeology and legacy of England between the fifth and eleventh centuries. Individual contributions question and situate key themes, and thereby bring new perspectives to the heritage of early medieval England. They draw on texts in Latin and Old English as well as material culture to paint a vivid picture of the period. Relevant not only to students and scholars working in medieval studies, these volumes explore the rich intellectual, methodological and comparative value that the dynamic researchers interested in England between the fifth and eleventh centuries have to offer in a modern, global context. The series is driven by a commitment to inclusive and critical scholarship, and to the view that early medieval studies have a part to play in many fields of academic research, as well as constituting a vibrant and self-contained area of research in its own right.

Cambridge Elements ⹋

England in the Early Medieval World

Elements in the Series

Printed in the United States
by Baker & Taylor Publisher Services